MY LIFE MY RULES

THULASI B RAMAN

Made with ♥ on the Notion Press Platform
www.notionpress.com

Contents

Preface

This book is dedicated to EVERYONE of us who believes in the word 'Magic' and wants Magic to be a part of our everyday life. This book will help everyone who wants to understand about Life in the simplest way possible. By mentally devouring its key attributes, we can prepare ourselves in ways that inherently take us in the direction of a growth mindset. While some of the individuals take Life for granted, others tirelessly moan and lament venting out their dissatisfaction about how difficult every moment is. From this it is very clear that there is no middle ground in the thinking patterns of people around the world. All of us as human beings have a tendency to desire for easier and quicker rewards with proportionally less effort.

I believe that to err is human. As we progress through the book, I have provided an insight into my experiences starting from my childhood up to the present. I hope to strike a chord with the readers using the book as a medium for my communication. This book is chiefly for those who are in the pursuit of an enriching and blissful experience. Once we get ready to embody the changes within ourselves as specified in the book, we are on the pathway to happiness. Living an effortless and effective life becomes the next logical step in our journey towards self-development. I take this opportunity to stress the fact that a productive and fulfilling life is easily achievable. We can *certainly* dare to dream and see it altering our existing situation.

In this book, I have penned my transformative journey from being a timid little girl to a proud woman who has accepted herself wholeheartedly and unabashedly, with all her flaws. I have given examples of my personal experiences that will help all of us appreciate the gift of Life that we have been showered and blessed with. My journey till date has been one of a kind. I suppose that every one of us gets to hear this same statement from all the authors. In my case, I have tried to be slightly different by not just journalling my personal experiences but also formulating the lessons that I have learnt along the way. The specific episodes that I have crafted hold a lot of importance personally as they have had a major influence in shaping my outlook.

Acknowledgements

I take this opportunity to pay gratitude to everyone who has been instrumental in shaping my life and teaching me its value through this book. Life is esoteric and deriving the valuable gems that it showers us with is nothing short of an adventure. I believe that there are no chance meetings, and everything is pre-destined. Every single person who I have come across and interacted with, has mentored me by just being a part of my sojourn. I am grateful to them for revealing to me the beauty of existence. I consider that all the occurrences that look like coincidences are the very lessons that have been sent across by the Universe to teach us the value of Life.

I would like to thank all the good as well as the overwhelming events that are integral to my growth for imparting priceless teachings in their own unique way. They have contributed significantly to my spiritual as well as materialistic enhancement and given me a new mental makeover.

I would like to first of all take the blessings of the Almighty and thank him for giving me the wisdom and intellect to write this book. I am grateful to my late parents who have done an excellent job of instilling the right values in my life. My parents have been a great support system to me and have constantly encouraged me in my aspirations. Their selfless service as doctors to lakhs of people inspired me a lot and gave me the courage to get ahead fearlessly onto the path of humanity. I have seen them providing tireless service to lakhs of people paying least attention to their own needs. As a child, seeing my parents work so passionately implanted the seeds of kindness and empathy within me.

I feel totally indebted and blessed to have a loving husband who guides me in all matters. His patience and resilience in looking after me when I lost both my parents helped me sail through the tough times with utmost ease. The interactions that I have had with my husband over a period of 16 years on innumerable topics have helped me grow immensely as a person with a touch of humanity. His humanitarian approach towards one and all is clearly reflected in his opinions and decisions. He has always been very understanding, fair and broad-minded. He always encourages me to think holistically while making decisions. His closer-to-reality approach makes it easy for me to be firmly grounded and take decisions rationally. I take this opportunity to specially thank my husband for always being there for me, no matter what. He is like a rock, who has stood by me at all times.

My nine-year old daughter is our angel and God's sweetest gift in our lives. Her cuteness and charm are beyond words. Her constant questions remind me of my childhood when I used to keep nagging my mom with endless questions about everything around me. Every day has been a learning as well as a challenging experience trying to provide her with the best possible abode for overall development. In fact, our bedtime interactions on every topic under the sun have been the main source of inspiration for this book. Her keen observations and understanding of certain facts in keeping with her age, have left me completely surprised on numerous occasions. Her queries have played a major part in fueling my idea about writing a book.

I am thankful to have the unwavering support of my in-laws in my journey. They have been a great source of encouragement till this date and have always given me the freedom to make my own decisions. They have been appreciative of my efforts in all my endeavors and have constantly nudged me to outperform myself. Their blessings and guidance have greatly impacted my understanding of life, giving me the necessary pointers required for writing this book.

My gratitude list will not be complete without mentioning my endearing and lovable sisters who have parented me in the best possible way when my parents were away for work. Both of them have always been very protective and caring towards me, thereby providing a safe haven for me. We share a close bond that is nurtured with lots of love and care for each other. They have been there for me at every stage of my Life and have pushed me to give my best in whatever I do.

My immense gratitude is due to my mentor, Abraham Hicks whose teachings has had a profound impact on my discernment. Just by listening to their podcasts, one feels hopeful and optimistic about Life. It was a chance encounter that I stumbled upon a recording of Abraham Hicks and since then there has been no looking back. By incorporating their teachings into my daily schedule, I have seen miraculous transformations in my quest for progress. It is easy to apply the practices given in their lectures without any radical changes to our existing setup.

In addition to this, the teachings of Neville Goddard have also been instrumental in helping me develop a positive mindset amidst testing times. The wisdom of the ages as delineated by Neville Goddard has had a significant impact on my thinking. It has opened my mental eyes to a larger and more beautiful world. I have realized that we need to be open to learn and receive. Once we are in the receiving state, our vessel will automatically start brimming with opulence and happiness. There is always light at the end of the tunnel – but it is up to us to be persistent enough to see the fruits of our hard work.

Introduction

Our dream life is just an arm's distance away from us and every one of us can make it our present day reality by adopting a small yet significant change in our attitudes. It is well within our reach to desire for precisely such miracles *provided* we are ready to make slight tweaks to our existing mindsets and lifestyle. We can undoubtedly attain the level of luxury and affluence envisioned by us thereby witnessing it take physical form in our reality.

All the circumstances in our lives imply only one main principle – Never Give Up on our deep-seated longings. The happenings around us may give the impression that there is nothing but hopelessness shrouding our path. It is just a fraction of a second that is required for everything to turn over. Though it may sound impracticable to be balanced in tough situations, keeping calm is the only way out of the most challenging phases. I have personally been through some of the most trying times and every episode has been a big learning in its own kind. All these incidents have been very crucial and were powerful enough to drive me towards a brighter future.

Nevertheless, there is more to these mind-boggling situations than meets the eye. The main takeaways from my testing periods were my increased self-belief and how well it helped in molding my mindset. I was in deep anguish and pain looking at my failures. I don't deny the fact that the change within me didn't come overnight. I am of the view that it is almost impossible for internal changes pertaining to our mind to take place drastically and suddenly. Though the decision to change can be made in a split second, it is the persistent effort taken in that direction that makes our entry into our dreamland the eternal truth. I am happy that my commitment to take the first step to change has borne fruit and revamped my spirit in a very positive way. I am cognizant that I have commenced my adventure with the right frame of mind but still have a long way to go.

I suppose that most of us will be able to relate to the emotions underlying the events that have been exclusively written for the benefit of all the readers. I have reasoned the ideologies of spirituality and societal norms from my viewpoint without getting into the nitty-gritties. This book draws the attention to the philosophy that being happy and flourishing on one's own terms (without causing harm and damage to others) is every person's birthright. The strategies that have been discussed in the following chapters can be put into practice with utmost ease. Happiness is a choice that we need to make, so that it opens the portal to a more liberating and enthralling life.

Most of us usually desire a satisfying, tension-free atmosphere for ourselves and our loved ones. We are under the impression that there are only a fortunate few who deserve such a blessing. We think that *those* people have been selectively chosen by the Supreme as their store of past merits is considerable. In the process, we consider ourselves undeserving and unlucky for no reason at all. We unnecessarily blame ourselves for our ill-fate. But honestly, this is not the case, and things can certainly be changed for the better. It all starts with just a thought – an impulse of thought to willingly integrate certain necessary modifications to our existing lifestyle.

I have pointed out the potential disservice we indulge in because of the unhealthy and debilitating thoughts that constantly envelopes our mind. It is during such times of adversities that we are challenged to hold on to our willpower and self-confidence so as to pursue our intended goal. In fact, we have the key to a successful and fantastic future right in our hands. However, unlocking the key to our joie de vivre requires that we incorporate clear-cut and simple changes in our everyday routine. A dedicated and continuous implementation of those changes makes all the difference. Adapting to these variations adds a bit of novelty and color to our existence.

I assume and hope that my book will be a source of comfort and will provide relief to millions of people in testing times. I have written this book with the sole intention of bringing a smile on every reader's face and giving them the assurance that everything is going to be okay. I am sure that the ideas delineated in the book will ease the minds of everyone reading it, particularly when everything seems dark. I am optimistic that by assimilating and blending the theories suggested in the book, we are bound to observe our lives, turning over a new leaf.

There are no complicated or laborious techniques presented here. On the contrary, the approaches that have been spoken at length in the book are straightforward and comprehensible. Every idea that has been talked through is practical and can be customized to our needs. We can easily integrate every one of the suggestions into our everyday routine, but it is *only* persistence that will yield us the fruits we expect. I would reiterate the authenticity and genuineness of the methods listed in the chapters which have had a magical effect on me.

There are many incidents that have been raised in this book that will remind us of how we handled our own situations. I have given a sneak-peek into my own encounters because of the eagerness to share my views about the diverse facets of Life. I am sure that some of the episodes highlighted will make us re-think our actions and put us into a self-analysis mode, while other instances may re-ignite the power within us and remind us of how resilient we were in trying situations. It is then that most of us become aware of how far we have successfully embarked in our trip till date. It is my strong belief that we are on an adventure, and it ought to be viewed that way.

I hope that this book will be able to strike a connection with individuals of every age group. I assume that as the book is read through, everyone will be re-living the past along with me. There are a number of golden nuggets that are hidden deep within each example that has been specified in the book. They can be explored as per the interest and keenness of the readers. As the chapters are concentratedly scanned through, the mysteries that were slowing our progress will be uncovered and unraveled. Once the mysteries begin to clear up, it will enable us to unmask and probe into the uncertainties that had played spoilsport in our plans up till now.

I would like to make a special mention that all the views that have been cited in this book are *entirely* from my perspective and based on my life experiences. This book is not written with a notion to offend or put anyone in a tight spot. This is a self-help book that will help all of us explore the beauty of life and appreciate its worth. At this juncture, I request the readers to take time to absorb the contents of the book slowly but steadily. The book can be put into practical use right at the point where we are in our expedition as of today. Reading this book will be inspire and help learn ways to go past the obstacles that have been hampering our growth until this moment. Once we are on the path to a glorious life, then there is no looking back.

CHAPTER ONE

Gift to Mankind

Life is a wonderful gift from the Universe to mankind. But how many of us really understand the meaning of this statement and vouch for it? That seems to be a pretty tricky question - does it not? Human Beings are the wonderful creations of God endowed with a special faculty called Knowledge which helps them to understand and perceive things rationally. This treasure of knowledge helps people make decisions by properly analyzing and calibrating the events at hand.

Every one of *us* is a masterpiece in the eyes of God - each with our own unique skills and talents. Then a question may arise in the minds of the readers that if we are the so-called precious gems created by the Universe, then why do pain and misery exist? How is it possible for abundance and agony to co-exist? How come there are only a lucky few who get to experience all the happiness and prosperity? What is so special about those *lucky few*? It is understandable that an existence that is steeped in poverty and sickness is a bane rather than a boon.

There are innumerable such questions that we come across in our daily encounters which make us ponder in silence. Many of us would have tried to figure out the answers to these queries by having countless discussions with our loved ones. A lot many times we feel that everything happening around us is unfair and biased especially when it comes to us but in reality, that is *never* the case. I was left numb when in spite of all my hard work and sleepless nights I didn't secure the grades I was expecting. The easiest response in such scenarios is to call out the system and I did the same. I felt that others were favored and believed in this accusation with all my heart. It did not strike me that there could be something lacking from my end. I was looking for reasons outside of me to answer my questions but never once took the *pain* to think from a different perspective and look within myself.

I now feel that I was not able to comprehend the situation at hand wisely and I mainly attribute this to my immaturity owing to my age. I was always of the opinion that I was being denied my rightful rewards by the Almighty despite all my efforts but much later realized that I was completely wrong. Most often, we jump to conclusions based on our lopsided understanding of the existing conditions. Yet, we rarely agree to the fact that we are being partial. How many of us have been in similar scenarios, and have accepted temporary defeat?

Life is known to engross us in endless issues to such an extent that we fail to notice the hidden benefits within those heart- wrenching moments. It is rightly said that the greatest challenges that stress us out are *blessings* in disguise because they reveal a side of our personality that we never knew *even* existed. Every day of my daily schedule is filled with tests from multiple, unexpected corners be it on the personal or professional front. The more we despise and try ways to avoid those trials, the more we find ourselves engulfed by them. Whenever I have tried to avoid the problems surrounding me, I have realized that it was a futile attempt from my end. In fact, doing so put me into a bigger turmoil that worsened my predicament. This is an axiomatic truth and there is no escape from it.

Every person is confronted with endless tribulations and facing them is the only solution to it. There are many such occasions where I have been cornered from opposing directions and balancing my responsibilities in such a context has been extremely difficult. Prioritizing the needs of everyone concerned effectively and taking decisions rationally has proved to be fruitful. I am pretty sure that most of us if not all endure similar ordeals day in and day out. I find myself tripping the balance quite often and holding myself in one piece despite the storm has been quite an achievement. Whenever I am at a crossroads and need to make a hard choice, I have followed my heart, and it has always proved me right in the long run. I do agree that some of my decisions have gone haywire and have not exactly given me the result I expected but nevertheless they have opened up a new path for me.

We need to believe and place our faith in the divine providence. We have heard our elders saying that ***'Everything happens for our own good'.*** I know that it sounds impracticable to conform to this advice, precisely when we are faced with roadblocks from all corners. When our plans come crashing down, we find it hard to keep ourselves together. I really found this saying mystical and unendearing especially when I failed to score exceptional grades. I thought to myself as to what good is buried in this incident but didn't talk about it to anyone. But years later, as I was sitting back and re-living my past, wonderful memories, I realized a strange thing. In particular, after that specific instance of low grades I dedicated more hours to gaining knowledge and planned my schedule well in advance to avoid any last-minute rush. I am not sure what motivated me to do this as I failed to take notice of the changes that were molding me as a person. My only focus was on my grades which had drastically improved, but I was unaware of the behind-the-scene picture that was on the works for my benefit.

In the process of going past hurdles after hurdles to reach our desired goal, we barely take note of the fact that we do learn a lot about ourselves along the way. The harsh reality is that we most likely overlook this eternal truth and focus only on the hardships. We are so busy spending our time nagging and bitching about our problems that it leaves us totally pinched off. It would be unfair on my part if I don't credit my growth to all the puzzles that have helped push my limits further. However, the truth is that we do have a face-off with ourselves as we proceed along our journey and that cannot be denied. Self-introspection helps us to be kind to ourselves and embrace ourselves with love. When we take a little effort to know ourselves, we are surely in for a surprise.

I was always intrigued by the vast economic divide existing in the world and the sufferings of people used to upset me a lot. I wondered how every person's state is so different as chalk and cheese if really everything in this Universe is fair? What can all of us do to alleviate this? A little prodding on my part brought to light an interesting piece of information that I would like to share with everyone. Every one of us on this planet is given the power of *freewill* to steer and control the direction of the path we wish to progress ahead in our travel. This means that we are in complete control of our well-being using our freewill and we can create our cherished reality.

Before we go ahead any further, let us try to understand the meaning of the term Freewill. **Freewill** is defined as the ability or capacity of human beings to make their own choices and create their own fates. That seems to be a pretty astonishing disclosure. Is it not amazing to know that we are the masters of our world and creators of our destiny?

"You are the creator of your own reality." - Esther Hicks

That sounds great – it is both good news as well as bad news. The fact that we can make the choices that best suit us gives us complete authority over ourselves. It means we are free to decide and select those options which fit in perfectly based on our requirements. Let us imagine a scenario where we are in the driver's seat of our favorite car. We are now given a chance to choose the route and the experiences along our journey. The thought itself is so powerful and immaculate that it is sure to give us goosebumps. The idea of feeling empowered makes us fall in love with our escapades all over again.

However, do we really enjoy and take delight in that enthusiastic feeling for a prolonged period of time? Or is our mind wandering elsewhere and chasing another dream in the interim? For the longest time, I was fervently chasing my dream career but as I was ardently pursuing this, something else turned up and I totally forgot about my long-lost wish. Life has a unique habit of providing its children with limitless and incredible opportunities that are beyond human imagination. Our thinking is limited and narrow in comparison to the infinite intelligence of the Supreme Power. We are never done with our desires as we revel in an expansive Universe where new dreams keep sprouting continuously. This unending surge of desires propels us to move ahead in excitement and thus make our endeavor all the more stimulating.

We need to be mindful of the fact that our passions and preferences keep altering based on our never-ending wants. There is not a single moment we refrain from thinking (except when we are asleep). Thinking is an involuntary process that goes on and on. As our thoughts keep fluctuating, so do our picks. But in a rush, to fulfill them we are forever chasing one dream after another. I now regret that I failed to celebrate my small successes along the way as I was busy planning the next move for another dream that I had already lined up. I say "small success" because once we achieve our set goal, we don't understand its worth. Aiming bigger and better is definitely not wrong but how do we justify the years of toil and sweat behind that one goal that had almost become an obsession. It didn't take a minute for me to shift my attention from my exceptional grades to discussions about applying for higher education. I completely forgot the tiring hours I had put in for the grades which were at one point my sole object of concentration let alone enjoying the wonderful moment with my family. All of us make such blunders now and then. We believe that we have less time in our hands and in that state of despair we fail to enjoy the essence of the present moment.

Every one of us is blessed with freewill and that attribute has been conferred on all of us in equal measure. But if we don't know how to use it effectively and correctly, we have no one but ourselves to blame. A person whose environment looks quite complicated and chaotic, can, at this *very* moment, make it simple. We can very well get things back on track by using our free will. It is just that a decision needs to be made in that direction and the will to stand by that conviction persistently. Nonetheless, things do not end merely with deciding, and getting back to our old self in the very next moment. On the contrary, sticking to *that* decision at all times no matter how difficult the going gets, is the one important factor that makes all the difference.

Now the question that crosses our mind right away is - why don't all of us follow this trail and make our habitats a happy haven of blessings? If it is that easy to create miracles in our Life as proclaimed, why is it not often put into practice by people? The answer to this secret will be revealed in the subsequent chapters.

CHAPTER TWO

LIFE AND SPIRITUALITY

We are all spiritual beings who have taken form in this physical world to enjoy the joyful and exhilarating experiences that the Cosmos has to offer us. However, this is in stark contrast to the beliefs I have been hearing and absorbing while I was growing up. Right from my childhood, I have always been taught that there is a higher power above all of us, whom most of us refer to as **GOD** (others call it *Source* or *Universe*). The idea that God is our sole owner and proprietor, who is in complete control of our destiny, was deeply rooted in me by my parents. I was born and brought up in an orthodox family with lots of importance being given to the concept of Supreme Power.

Most of us will agree that the concepts of God and spirituality were often taught in a manner that normally instilled a sense of fear in our mind in olden days. The ideas of fear and punishment were constantly ingrained into our innocent minds lest we try to cross the line. I have constantly heard people around me telling that by not living in accordance with the rules of the society, we are putting ourselves at risk and thereby disrespecting God. Though there has been substantial change in the way these ideologies are approached in modern times, I am of the opinion that we still have a long way to go. As far as spirituality is concerned, from a very young age, our brains are programmed in such a way that the emotion of fear dominates our minds. Our lives are based on a strong belief system that has now become a part of our entity as well as our personality.

"The Law of Life is the Law of Belief." – Joseph Murphy

I found this theory quite intimidating *as well as* silly. I still remember my innocence and ignorance with regards to the matter. I used to question my mom endlessly about everything under the sun with a twinkle in my eyes. My questions ranged from theories of spirituality and God to conditions of poverty and affluence. I always thought to myself that if God is so loving and the One as claimed, then why is it that hard-working people suffer incessantly. However, my persistence in understanding the basis and rules of the society was met with cold and blunt behavior from my mom. This further intrigued me, making me agitated and piquing my curiosity in knowing more.

Most of us must have closely observed our parents' unconditional labor and countless hours at work in order to fulfill that one special wish which we had expressed to them in our childhood. I still clearly remember my dad dedicating extra time at work so that he could surprise me with a gift just in time for my birthday. As a kid though I did not understand much about the ways of world, I noticed that there was a constant pressure clearly visible on my parents' face. I didn't know what it was then and tried to dig in deep to find out what was bothering them but was welcomed with the usual snub. There had been times where I literally did what I was told, unwillingly and half-heartedly. Whenever I had tried to emulate my elders blindly without being able to relate to the situation at hand, there was an underlying feeling of reluctance within me that made me slightly cold at times.

The more I tried fitting into the norms of the society, the more I got lost in the crowd. I failed to understand what was occurring around me. The ambience seemed quite blurred and suffocating. I tried to find out and reason things using my logic. I found something was amiss but did not know what it was. I had a strange gut feeling that things and events were not syncing up in the way they should. I could not articulate my emotions properly and due to the earlier silencing from my mom, I quieted myself. I felt that it is better that I keep my doubts to myself instead of bothering my parents.

The unanswered questions and confusions were taking the form of suppressed emotions within me. Amidst all this, I was fighting my emotions all alone in reticence. The stage was set - it was my thoughts vs the belief system. There was a wide gap between my thoughts and the beliefs that I grew up with, making it perplexing for me to lead a normal life. Logical reasoning not just failed but actually made matters worse for me. I think that every one of us has been at this place at least once in our time and will surely be able to relate to me.

Every one of us has our own share of ups and downs which we battle within our minds with the fear of being judged. Every phase for a human being is not just important in its own way but also brings with it limitless difficulties. Every thought, every change and every battle begins in our mind. Our mind is like a garden, and it is up to us to plant the right seeds to reap a rich harvest. By consciously thinking the right, productive thoughts, we can be assured of a mentally healthy atmosphere. Richness in Life is not just confined to wealth and money per se. Being successful is one that is copious in every sense – mentally, spiritually and financially.

"What you focus on, grows." – Esther Hicks

Let us suppose that we constantly dread the idea of being judged. In this case, the easiest approach to keep oneself apace with society would be to play safe by being tongue-tied. That is exactly what I did when I was brimming with doubts galore. I didn't want to get on the wrong side of my parents and earn their displeasure. I thought that being tight-lipped was the best bet for me as there was no fear of my ideas being unheard. By doing so, we claim to defend ourselves from needless poking and unwarranted mockery. But is this actually the right approach? Does keeping mum solve the impending problems or is it just an alternative to safeguard ourselves? What effects do these have in the long run? I guess these are some of the most prevalent queries that we come across in our daily errands. As we move on, we will get a clearer picture of how to control and manage such scenarios.

With no feminist stand being taken, it is unfortunately true that the society is by far, way more stringent when it comes to girls and women. Being born in a family of girls, I have been through all of this, and I understand the finer nuances much better. I was the youngest in the family and looked up to my sisters for *literally* everything. I was taught not to toe the line and just follow the rulebook set by my parents. Whenever I was dissatisfied and not entirely convinced with my mom's explanation, I used to discuss it with my sisters until I was convinced. This reminds me of my share of arguments that I had with my sisters on topics that seemed frivolous and incomprehensible to me. They felt that I was unnecessarily inviting trouble for myself by questioning the system. It was their way of protecting and shielding me from unwarranted criticism which never came to light then.

However, these aspects about society paint an altogether different picture from the one which we saw in Chapter 1 – Gift to Mankind. If Life is the gift which we have been showered with, why is it so cumbersome to even breathe easily? Why do most of us survive just because we have to? I am sure that every one of us has felt this pinch at some stage and point. At times, we find ourselves entwined in meaningless and rudderless conditions with no proper anchor. Are we under the illusion that the going is tough on us, and we need to endure this pain all through our life span for no fault of ours? Or is it really *as miserable* and difficult as it seems to us?

Despite planning things well in advance and taking the necessary precautions, I sometimes feel that I am in the midst of a hurricane that will wash me out any moment. I get dumb struck, and my mind goes blank at such times. Every single move that I make to get out of the pit seems to backfire and puts me into newer problems. When I start to solve a problem by fixing it from one end hoping for a quick resolution, I am left shell-shocked at the innumerable loopholes that the current solution has unveiled. These problems pull me further down and open up a box of unexpected riddles that test me further.

If I am in the middle of fixing and helping my daughter with her work, out of nowhere we are surmounted with a household issue that we never saw coming that calls for a huge expense. Arranging the necessary funds and getting the situation in place to curtail the newly erupted problem becomes the immediate goal to be achieved. Such moments are spent in lots of anxiety where I lose my self-confidence and self-worth. Tiring situations like these are common for everyone and strangely no one is spared. I feel that no amount of preparation helps and being on our toes is the best way to face such a crisis. So, what do we do about this?

The answer to all these questions lies in the superpower of freewill that is bestowed on every individual on this planet without any discrimination. *But* unfortunately, it is rarely put to use as most of us don't even realize that it exists, and it is well within our reach. This sounds unbelievable, doesn't it? This is the harsh truth and the reality for 98% of the people. Most of us think that any incident occurring is happening *to* us – be it trauma, pain, heartbreak etc. In all the confusion that envelopes us, the major point that we tend to miss is - everything is happening *for* us and is being planned out in our favor. As a matter of fact, all the events are being orchestrated perfectly by the Universe for our own personal and spiritual growth.

CHAPTER THREE

CONCEPT OF FREEWILL

It is rightly said that we are on an outing on this planet and there is no precise destination per se. All of us have taken birth in this physical world to enjoy, learn and grow from the experiences that are showered upon us. It is true that unless we imbibe the wisdom gained from those tests and put that knowledge into practice, we will not be able to appreciate the worth of our existence. Life needs to be studied, analyzed and thought through as a concept. A single incident does not define a person. On the contrary, it is all the events occurring over the entire span of a person on the Earth that sum up the personality of an individual because every little incident is a teaching in itself.

"Life is a journey, not a destination." - Ralph Waldo Emerson

Is it not startling why certain specific patterns keep recurring to us? – the angry boss, the relatives who keep questioning us endlessly on topics we are not comfortable with, the traffic we encounter whenever we step out on the road that gets on our nerves etc. to name a few? Have we ever tried to probe the circumstances and investigate them further? If not yet, then let us do it right now.

Let's take a moment to focus and ponder on what is actually happening in the background. Many of us end up working for an angry and nagging boss in spite of changing many companies. I have found myself getting time and again into situations that I always wanted to avoid. I have repeatedly faced the constant ranting of my seniors and have had to work with manipulative colleagues in office. Steering clear of office politics is a skill that I regret not learning at the right time for which I had to pay a heavy price. Time and again I have observed that despite my soulful longing to work in an atmosphere filled with optimism and positivity, I eventually find myself collaborating with people who talk behind our backs.

Similar to this is the case where we are welcomed with the endless waiting time and non-stop honking in traffic *almost* every single day. It has been a long time since we as a family did not have to re-schedule our plans whenever we set out for an outing due to the streams of vehicles on the road. If at all we are lucky enough that everything turns out in our favor, all our expectations with regards to the trip takes a toll in the wake on an unexpected accident. These are but few of the experiences that most of us must have run into. Frustration, irritation and complaining are some of the most natural reactions that one expects from an individual in these situations. It is very common to feel let down and knocked out in such conditions.

However, let us try to examine these frequent episodes from a slightly different point of view. Instead of being pessimistic and despondent, a little effort on our part to scrutinize the present state of affairs can help us garner huge benefits. By inspecting why certain *special* events are commonplace we can literally turn the events around at that very moment. We will be able to know if it is a coincidence that things are lining up the same way every single time or is it our misfortune?

I believe that it is easier said than done when the whole world appears to be against us. In fact, it takes lots of patience to step back, pause and *actually* start observing the surroundings. Self-control helps greatly in these places when the easiest instinct is to outrightly jump into action-mode at the first instance. The core idea is to remain a silent spectator for a few moments before reacting. Calming oneself down helps to assess the situation in a much better way. Decisions taken on the spur of the moment most likely result in mishaps and future regret.

A strange phenomenon of our term on Earth which is clothed under circumstances is that, unless we have learnt our lessons, we are bound to face the same situations again and again. Life is a teacher that tests us and continuously molds us into the best version of ourselves. It is ironic that we are so involved in fighting our day to day battles continually that we fail to look beyond our tiny problems. This leaves us with no scope and energy for any expansion – material or spiritual. To our utter disbelief and shock, we realize one fine day that we are exactly at the same spot. Suddenly, all our years of struggle and pushing through seem meaningless. We observe that we have moved not an inch ahead or an inch behind. If that is the case, how are we to fare then? Is there any prospect for us to move forward happily and rely on the chance events that are laid out before us?

It is here that the effective use of the concept of freewill helps us face our inner demons confidently and effortlessly, thereby shaping us into far better and matured individuals. As stated previously, freewill is a tool that helps us to route and re-route our life, time and again in the direction we wish to proceed. It is at our disposal to use it to our advantage as part of our daily rituals and experience the changes right away.

"If you don't write your Destiny, your Situation will do it for you."

'As you sow, so shall you reap' is an age-old proverb that every one of us must have heard from our parents and teachers. This proverb clearly teaches us that we reap the harvest of those seeds that we sow. Is it possible that we sow the seeds of thistles and expect to reap a harvest of grains? The answer is a clear- No. If we are able to understand the gist of this proverb in its true sense, it will help us hugely. This proverb holds good in every case and by effectively applying it whenever the occasion demands, we can learn our valuable lessons in a less painful way. By doing this, happiness becomes our natural state of mind and magic seems realistic *all of a sudden*. We start to wonder why everything is working in our favor all of a sudden and it even feels bizarre. We question ourselves as to where was *this happiness* hidden in all these lean years?

Beating the drum of pain and agony with a victim mentality will do us no good. It not only discourages us even more but also stops us from blooming. It is here that the super powerful freewill comes in handy. Freewill gives us the power of decision-making. The moment we **decide** to analyze and learn from a specific incident that is continually putting us off is the *turning point* in the game of our Life. Once we begin to look into the instances closely, we come across certain hidden facts that unleashes the knot. It is *precisely* then that every single aspect pertaining to us starts to change for the better. It is this *decision* to make and be the change, that makes all the difference. Freewill is the game changer that gives us a sense of freedom and exhilaration.

"And one day I understood that it is no one's job,

but Mine, to take care of myself and make myself happy." - Paulo Coelho

Taking a step back and pausing allows us to calm ourselves for the moment. It is this calmness that takes us towards clarity and provides answers to our so-called self-created mayhem. Once we have a clearer picture of the scene at hand, we will be in full control of the situation. We can emphatically put forth our views in crisp and clear words without hurting the other person. This way we can be assured of avoiding any unwarranted outbursts and emotional turmoil. There are immeasurable occasions wherein we may be in the vicinity of people who we are not very comfortable with. This fact is true in both our personal and professional circle – something that cannot be denied. When talking through the matters doesn't pay dividends, the one best favor we can do on ourselves is to ignore such people as much as possible. In those cases where ignoring the group or an individual is not possible, we can definitely keep to ourselves and get away once the work at hand is completed.

Initially I was not aware of handling people at office who made things quite strenuous for me. Most of the times, I was at the receiving end and that pushed me to the wall. Introspecting facilitates us to discover our hidden qualities in a far better way and paves way for change whenever it is essential. Gradually I learnt to tackle the gossipmongers by just being physically available for them. Mentally, I was elsewhere – concentrating on my other priorities and deadlines that were far more important to me both at work and at home. It is just a mindset shift that makes all the difference and inspires us farther in our expedition. The second I decided that these special people don't need to be given so much importance turned the tables for me. I chose not to give in to their tantrums and that fixed my tensions.

It is not **required** that we react and get enraged at every incident that irritates us. Sometimes the best way would be to just let it go and distract us. If the traffic and honking infuriate us, then the best option would be to plug in the earphones and enjoy soulful music. I do understand that in all the commotion around us, many of us may be skeptical if this suggestion makes any sense. Though this may not be the best of the solutions for the situation at hand, I can for sure guarantee that this at least lessens our irritation to some extent. I have tried doing this and this has for sure helped me. If we are by ourselves in our vehicle, listening to podcasts or interviews as per our likings not just distracts us from the chaos we are in, but it also helps us gain knowledge.

"When you complain, you make yourself a victim. Leave the situation. Change it or Accept it. All else is madness." - Eckhart Tolle

By using the powerful tool of freewill appropriately, life becomes a cake walk. We need to develop this habit and use it to our advantage. Abundance follows logically in our ride towards empowerment. It takes lots of courage and willpower to make decisions – which means that using our ability of freewill is, no doubt, initially difficult. I agree that it is no mean feat to shed our older self and incorporate new beliefs. Nevertheless, by regularly and systematically making them our daily habit, we gain confidence and self-control. While some may find it easy to use, others may require continued efforts to see even small, noticeable changes. Once we start to observe the positive changes around us, we are motivated to reach the next level of richness and opulence soon.

CHAPTER FOUR

Acceptance of Oneself

As a kid, I was shy, silent and a total introvert. I was never comfortable speaking in public and looked for opportunities to escape from large crowds. I always used to feel safe in the comfort zone that I had created for myself in my mind and would rarely entertain anyone into it. I had a very small circle of friends *with only* whom I was comfortable sharing my secrets and ideas. I always wondered about my silent nature and why was it so tough for me to gather courage before an audience? I could hardly engage in a conversation and not feel the discomfort. Even if I went to parties, I hardly spoke to anyone in the social gathering and was always eager to get back home. I loved reading books and enjoyed spending time with myself. I had a lot of mood swings and depending on my mood, I engaged in hearty conversations with my close friends.

I remember being heckled and ridiculed for not knowing how to ride a two-wheeler, but it seldom mattered to me. I had fallen off a vehicle and had scratches all over my body. I was very excited at the prospect of riding a bike for the first time in my life but was disappointed a lot. I decided not to venture into this any time soon and let things take their own course. Though the idea of learning driving from a professional popped up in my mind every now and then, I kept postponing it telling myself that the right time hadn't arrived yet. The entire incident seemed quite simple, but now when I give it a thought, that is not the case.

As we proceed through this chapter, the matters will become much clearer, and the curtains will be opened to deeper aspects. I never once understood that just thinking about dreams and aspirations alone is not enough, but it needs to culminate into action. Sadly, my right time to become a confident driver has not arrived till date. Initially, everything felt perfect as per my likes. But as I was growing up, I *felt* that something was not alright, and I had to take some action but stopped myself like always. I shut off the voice within me and ignored the calling completely. I had a strange nudge that something was awry but failed to acknowledge it.

As I look back and try to connect the dots, I now understand that it was *actually* my fear of stepping into the unknown that I was refusing to give heed to. The reason being that it would require me to do things which were out of my safe zone. I believed that they were NOT part of my personality. An unknown territory expects us to take action in areas that challenge us and requires us to embrace a newer perspective. If I had mustered the courage to learn driving at any cost when the rod was hot, things would have panned out so differently. Once a situation cools off, neither the drive nor the intensity of the urge to fulfill a deeply seated dream remains the same.

At this point I am drawn to discuss another such episode that holds relevance. There was this particular incident that occurred in my teens that literally shook me and had a great impact on me. I still remember the awkwardness and the feeling of being mocked when I failed to deliver my debate speech properly while in school. I was criticized heavily for being too fast while speaking, swallowing some words and not being able to strike a rapport with the onlookers. For an individual who barely used to speak out, participating in a debate competition itself seemed like a big achievement. My situation can be likened to expecting a toddler to run in a race and also win the trophy when I could barely crawl.

I resented the listeners and felt that they were too harsh *only* on me. I convinced myself in no uncertain terms that they had played favoritism and on purpose put me down. All of us would agree that this incident is detrimental and quite difficult for a teenager to handle. Undoubtedly, it has the power to sabotage one's confidence and self-esteem, if allowed to do so. Likewise, my first response was one of self-sabotage and shutting myself off completely from everyone around me. It was my illusion that every person in the crowd was my so-called enemy and I blocked them off from my line of sight completely. This is a very natural response of a person who is not very comfortable opening up before others.

I had dusted off the 'two-wheeler' incident as unimportant and insignificant. But frankly, it had successfully planted a seed of fear and criticism deep in my mind which I was not aware of back then. Similar to it was the 'debate' incident which reaffirmed that fear and made me critical of myself. The incidents that I have mentioned above are quite akin to one another as both of them stealthily work on the psyche of an individual. Self-criticism is a major roadblock in a person's life as it never allows us to progress peacefully and brings on needless mental conflicts.

"Your opinion of yourself is your most important viewpoint. You are infinitely greater than you think you are." - Neville Goddard

Being a teenager is one of the most challenging and tricky phases for a person. The experiences that one faces in that age get permanently etched in one's mind. Whenever I see my daughter's urge to put her foot into newer, completely off-track avenues, I am left baffled. As I closely observe her actions, I have realized that kids rarely fear criticism unless there is more to it than meets the eye. Most of the times, teenagers and particularly children have the innate ability to explore and are courageous as they don't dread judgement from others. As parents it is our responsibility to harness this in-born skill in the right direction whenever the occasion demands. Though it has been my initial tendency to protect my daughter from any harm and failure, I learnt it the hard way that I am doing her no good by being this over-possessive parent. I greatly credit my husband for helping me have an open mind and be a spectator at times. In fact, by stopping children from experimenting various choices we are actually cutting off their wings and also expecting them to soar to greater heights – both at the same time.

It would be wrong to say that I was perfectly okay after that *particular* nerve-wrecking debate incident. In fact, I had spent many sleepless nights writhing in pain and guilt, trying to actually interpret what had happened with me. This is just one of the many instances which people experience. Most of the times, our present-day actions have a connection with our past memories that may seem irrelevant at this moment, but those memories are safely guarded in our hearts as an unhealed wound. It is well-known that a child's mind is a sponge that absorbs every single emotion perfectly in the same proportion as it is delivered. Keeping this important point in mind, it is highly necessary that the right content should be assimilated by children lest it plays havoc at a later period.

Scathing incidents such as the ones I have mentioned are quite common for every individual. No one is lucky enough to be spared from the heat.

The victims end up suffering in silence for fear of criticism and doom. Unfortunately, not a single person other than the victim is aware of the torrent that has come in knocking. It was not that my family members were less caring or not empathetic, but I would rather say that I was not in the right frame of mind to open up to them. I expected them to only be a silent listener to my woes and not advise me, at least for the time being. All of us know that people listen to speak and not to understand a situation. Knowing very well that there are chances of me being advised or reprimanded which I was in no mood to listen to, I decided to keep to myself.

There are many of us around the world like me who despite sharing an intimate and understanding bond with our family and friends choose silence as the best weapon to regret over our losses. So, it becomes all the more important that we try to learn what needs to be done when such nasty things happen to us or our close ones. Whenever it seems to us that Life is tossing us ruthlessly for no fault of ours, it means that we are being nudged to do something different – something more. Sometimes we find ourselves embroiled in an incessant storm, and it is during such testing times that we are shaped into the best versions of ourselves. It took me literally years to get out of the ordeal and make peace with the situation. So, what does making peace with a situation mean? Does it mean that we accept whatever has happened to us as our fate and whine in stoic silence? Or do we pretend that we have forgotten everything and move on happily as if we are unaffected by our bumpy ecosystem? Surely, not.

All of us are heaped with benefits and we are here to experience the beauty of the Cosmos to the fullest. Accepting oneself with one's flaws without being judgmental is the first step towards a stress-free life. This means that we should be open and willing to learn from our mistakes without being rigid. Self-acceptance is the key to a better self-concept. Only if we are able to love and accept ourselves the way we are, can we expect the same from others. Self-doubt and a sense of unworthiness only make things difficult for us. They not only add to our existing woes but also worsen our plight.

I believe that being imperfect is perfectly okay as long as we don't beat ourselves up for it. We need to be cognizant that we are creatures having a soul filled with emotions. When our focus is on *being perfect* in everything we do, we become robots. By doing so, we begin to invite unwarranted stress for ourselves because of the impossible nature of this endeavor. We no longer enjoy the time at hand and are forever in a race. Trying to be perfect at every single point of time, eventually, becomes demanding and burdensome.

The emotions of the past are still afresh in my mind but now with the power of my free will, I am able to consciously direct my thoughts that help bring the best out of me. I do get bogged down sometimes but remind myself *every day* of how far I have come. Instead of cursing and hating myself for my past mistakes, I now know that the best way to rectify them is to take responsibility for my actions. I now believe - all thanks to my blunders that there is nothing like waiting for the right time. Our gut feeling or intuition, by whatever name we call it, is the best and most effective emotional guidance tool at our disposal. Recognizing the emotions at the first instance and being observant act as useful pointers to re-route our thoughts. Refusing to accept our feelings and shooing them away will only lead us to a vicious circle of negativity. Whenever the mind is flooded with past trials, the best way to get over them is to allow the stifled thoughts to freely flow. It is well known based on the Law of Action and Reaction that the more we bottle up our emotions, the more it will affect us emotionally and mentally.

"When you focus on the good, the good gets better." - Esther Hicks

When we allow thoughts to freely flow with no resistance, it means that we are ready to face the problem head-on. We become ready to face a problem only if at first place we accept that there is an issue. The foremost mistake I made was to deny having any issues followed by burying my emotions whenever they cropped up. It is no surprise for everyone reading this chapter to predict my state of affairs. When the burden that we unknowingly carry on our shoulders becomes too heavy to pull on, it is then that we begin to look for alternative solutions. It was precisely at one such moment that I luckily came across a video on Freewill that raised a hope in the darkness I had thrust myself into.

As stated in Chapter 3 – Concept of Freewill, cultivating the habit of a mindset shift and being open to admit our faults (if any) opens up an obstacle-free path before us. As humans we are bound to trip in almost every sphere we could never even imagine. Nevertheless, only when we graciously proceed by learning and rectifying our faults can we expect to be successful. Evolving from our blunders and trying to improve through our setbacks is the key factor that helps us stand out in a crowd.

Initially, I kept questioning my lack of confidence in presenting my ideas to others and was on a repeated self-sabotage process. Years later when by a chance encounter I took notice of the unnecessary load I was holding without my knowledge, I felt that it was high time I just let it go. To begin with, I stopped resenting and being spiteful with all *those* people who had scorned me. It was the most opportune moment for me when I did that, as it relieved me of all hurtful emotions. I felt free and light after a very long time as I had emptied myself of all the unnecessary baggage. Though at my low times, I do re-visit these painful situations, the frequency of my visits has considerably reduced. Once I released the ill-feelings, I began upskilling myself. I started to keenly observe the way everyone communicated and catered specific time to learn effective ways to speak defiantly. Though the entire process has been quite long and tedious, I am proud of the way I have evolved as a person – i.e. understanding and empathetic.

Family and friends play a vital role in an individual's self-growth journey. Being able to confide our emotions and feelings in someone we trust can bring in the much needed clarity quickly. Sharing our pain and thoughts with our near and dear eases the mind instantly. It cannot be denied that family members and friends know us much better and can efficiently help us to handle such situations with panache. Being surrounded by compassionate people ensures that our journey is meaningful as it boosts our self-confidence to higher levels.

CHAPTER FIVE

Secret to Happiness

When self-acceptance becomes a part of our personality, peace and happiness follow it. All of us know that our face is considered to be a mirror to the inner thoughts reeling in our mind. A happy face reflects a joyful and peaceful inner-being. When we start to concede and acknowledge ourselves, our focus is immediately shifted to the idea of self-development. We stop giving our energy to self-criticism and consequently, self-sabotage is left far behind. Our entire time is productively spent on finding ways and means to improve ourselves rather than moaning in regret.

A healthy mind is like fertile soil that yields the best results even in challenging weather conditions. The next question that automatically arises is - what is a healthy mind? We all know that one can have a healthy body but what does it mean to have a healthy mind? A mind brimming with thoughts of positivity, exhilaration and prosperity is considered healthy and fertile. By depositing critical and hateful thoughts in our mind, we are indeed digging up the soil of our mind intermittently and planting thorns in it. Doing this over and over again makes the land (in this case, our mind) barren. If, on the contrary, we carefully and intentionally fill our minds with notions of hope, expectation and anticipation, the results we obtain will be entirely different.

"Happiness is the harvest of a quiet mind." – Joseph Murphy

Self-acceptance and self-love are the doorways to happiness. If we are able to love ourselves unconditionally, there is nothing like it. We tend to forget how amazing and special we are amidst the unseen race we engage ourselves in. We don't need to search and find reasons to start adoring ourselves. It can be done right away and at this *very moment*. Self-love is the purest form of gratitude that we can show God for his wonderful creation. Once we embrace ourselves wholeheartedly despite our shortcomings, we unknowingly develop empathy towards our fellow human beings. Ideas of progress and self-development are always on our minds, and we are filled with enthusiasm. This moves us constantly in the direction of growth and well-being.

"Change your conception of yourself and you will automatically change the world in which you live." - Neville Goddard

Our minds become devoid of low vibration and negative emotions as we stop fueling it with our old thinking patterns anymore. We start to feel light in our heads as if a big burden is lifted off our shoulders. Just as I had mentioned in Chapter 4 - Acceptance of Oneself, the point of time I released the burden of hate and frustration that I was holding tight in my heart akin to a top secret against my critics , I could feel the difference in no time. I felt that I had done a big favor on myself by admitting that I had for sure committed mistakes in the competition and fixing them is no big deal. I experienced a sense of serene calmness after a very long battle with myself that cannot be put into words.

The idea of perfection is altered to fit in a more realistic person. Once we consent to this thought, we become kind and gentle towards ourselves. The self-created, illusive, perfect picture which we were living in our fantasy world is replaced with a cheerful one that is much less demanding. It becomes easier to explore the world at our own pace. This does not mean that we become lazy and sluggish procrastinating every goal that is on our list. Alternately we should pursue our goals with renewed strength and focus better by using our new-found wisdom. I would like to elaborate further by citing certain scenarios that are relevant in this context.

All of us are very well aware that weekdays are normally packed with loads of work, especially when we have children in our households. There is a constant tiff and an underlying race against time that mostly all of us experience. There are many a times when it gets extremely difficult for me to get my daughter ready to school on time owing to her tantrums, especially in the mornings when I already have a packed schedule glaring at me. Despite repeatedly preparing her well in advance the previous night and even requesting her to keep her behavior in check, the results are far from my expectations. The first few days of her school when she had just got enrolled put me in a quandary.

I had planned out every single detail well in advance and was all the more excited to see my plans come into fruition. I wanted to be *this perfect* mother and superhero who could juggle all tasks easily and effortlessly. Only when I actually got into action, did I realize how difficult it would have been for my mom with three children at home. I am of the view that most parents would advocate my thoughts. I found myself at a point which was so very different from the movie I had been playing in my head all this while. The more I tried to straighten things out and push others to forcefully fit into my perfect plan, the worser it got. It took me a while to actually comprehend the damage I had done by putting everyone concerned in a tight spot due to my obsession and craze to be perfect in all my doings.

Luckily, the intensity of damage was well within limits, and I set about on my mission of damage control. I stopped being unrealistic and irritable. I started to engage my daughter in fun games for a little while to such an extent that she was cheerful and very happy in the peak mornings. She stopped being stubborn and in the interim I got my work done as well. It was a win-win situation. It may at first sight seem foolish to sit and engage in fun talks with kids, especially when our mornings are jam-packed. I am fully aware that all of us have busy schedules, but joyous mornings are a much better and bigger bet than straining our relationship with the children for our interests. By planning our schedules better and being flexible to incorporate changes whenever needed, this is definitely achievable.

The moment we are okay with our plans not transpiring exactly the way we had envisioned; we give room for a whiff of fresh air to enter the premises i.e. our mind. Freewill helps greatly in such conflicting states and gives us the courage to choose our route practically. It opens up newer avenues for us and never lets us give up. It teaches us to be hopeful and just keep moving on, no matter what. Despite all the ruckus I had caused, I never actually felt totally let down and was all the more willing to fix my mistakes. It is this intention that makes all the difference - the amount of time to get the expected outcome slowly begins to lose its significance once we make up our mind.

I believe that we spend a larger portion of our valuable time thinking about how others perceive us. When we create an image of being worthless in our minds about ourselves, it is assured that we will be treated in the same way by others. If we ourselves feel less deserving and not enough, how can we expect others to appreciate us? We need to understand that every single emotion experienced inside our minds gets reflected in our day to day activities. The emotions deeply impressed in our minds work as the cause while the evidence seen in the form of incidents transpiring, turns out to be the effect.

By sowing the seeds of low self-esteem and disbelief within us, we end up getting entwined into circumstances that question our mettle time and again. As humans all of us make this flaw unknowingly. There are many such days where I am low on energy and mood. Keeping up with the need and speed of the hour becomes highly taxing in such cases. I feel completely drained out and look upon myself as a total wash out despite the continued efforts. A sense of uncertainty and self-doubt fills my mind. It is well-known that our thoughts dictate our actions. Having a bad mood shows up clearly in my actions and like a domino effect, things take a downward turn uncontrollably. There is every chance that at such times we end up making more mistakes. That may put us into places where we may have to prove our worth often that further affirms our self-doubts.

" The world is a mirror, forever reflecting what you are doing within yourself." - Neville Goddard

It is at this point that self-love comes to our rescue and becomes our savior. When we constantly regurgitate to ourselves about how beautiful, skilled and talented we are, we begin to slowly develop a special and divine connection with our inner self. That is the *most* propitious moment when everything begins to work for us and living becomes pure, ineffable joy. We need to consistently and consciously gauge our thoughts to redirect them along the right path. This way we will be able to understand how the concept of self-love operates.

Thinking is an activity that happens automatically in the background but that holds the key to our success. If I begin to take notice of why at first place things fell apart on a particular day, I am left in for a shock. I realize that I was preoccupied with thoughts about my other unfulfilled commitments that were bothering me. The dissatisfaction at my progress with respect to that commitment surged out as an irritation on a miniscule folly occurring at the present moment. This is a classic example of cause and effect that spoils our whole day.

If we take charge of our emotions at the right time, we will be well-aware of when situations are going out of hand. By being in complete control of the situation we can make the appropriate changes to better the ambience using our freewill power. This has got more to do with inner work and cleansing our minds of ill-feeling impressions about oneself. This is way different from setting and achieving tangible goals like jobs, relationships etc. that we are normally accustomed to where the results are clearly visible.

Self-love doesn't mean we get totally absorbed into ourselves and forget all our other responsibilities. On the contrary, self-love is just a gentle reminder about the responsibility we have towards our TRUE SELF. When we start to practice self-love assiduously, we become calm, forgiving and humble human beings. Initially all this may seem to be a sham and even sound weird. We may even feel that we are being selfish by prioritizing ourselves over our closed ones. Mostly in all of our homes, we have always been schooled to keep others' interests over ours. Does this mean that we ignore our likes and dislikes? Is it wrong to think about ourselves *first*?

People who would like to argue and criticize fail to understand the crux of the whole subject. I surely don't encourage that we become self-obsessed in the name of self-love. Self-love is a form of self-care that is highly essential for our soul. As we slowly start being gentle with ourselves, our eyes are opened to those hidden dimensions of our personality that leave us in awe of ourselves. Spreading unalloyed joy and happiness to everyone becomes our true goal. We become eager to share our stories of self-discovery with our loved ones hoping to inspire them as well. Mindless ego clashes and personal disputes no longer interest us as they look meaningless with no value added.

Once gaiety sets in, a closer scrutiny reveals that all the obstacles and hurdles that were blocking our way, get cleared off on their own with little or no effort. We are able to easily achieve our goals. A well-maintained work-life balance becomes a living reality. How did this *magic* happen all of a sudden? The truth is that **this Magic** always existed, it is just that we failed to admit its presence and pay heed to it. It is nothing but the magical genie of happiness that I am talking about. What exactly is happiness and how do we make it an indispensable entity of our lives?

Happiness is nothing but a state of mind that begins with just an impulse. What exactly is *that* impulse? It is the thought of being jubilant and doing whatever it takes to make it our sustained feeling. The moment we decide to *let go* of the absolute need to exercise control on every aspect within our reach we have won half our battle. The other half is won and will give us the expected results when we are willing to release the overwhelming, undermining thoughts that no longer serve us. Developments begin to take a drastic positive turn and everything lines up for our best when we begin to find contentment in every little detail of our routine.

Let us not let circumstances control and dictate our future. If we think that only after achieving a particular goal, we are going to be happy then that is never going to happen. This is because, once we get to our goal, we have something exciting already lined up as our new target. As cited in Chapter 1 - Gift To Mankind, I literally forgot about my grades and how well I had performed in my exams once the results were announced as my next object of attention was already in queue. We are never going to get done with our dreams and ambitions as this is an inclusive Universe.

But what good is there in attaining success after success in every task that we fixate ourselves on, if we are all the time anxious, tensed and worried? Is it going to help us in any way? I do agree that getting apprehensive is quite natural and totally permissible provided we know where to draw the line. It is my viewpoint that we need to calibrate and evaluate our emotions cautiously so that they don't go overboard. Mindfulness about the way we feel and react to situations can aid us in improving ourselves. We can assuredly use our power of freewill and avoid any unexpected flare-up that would otherwise result in a catastrophe.

Most of us have heard people rightly saying - 'Go with the flow', especially when we are confused to make any critical decisions. The main intent behind the phrase 'Go with the flow' is as we carry on our worldly duties with *complete faith* in the Source, a track will open up that will be for our own benefit. I have experienced this fact to be true in my own case where in dire circumstances I was left with no option but to surrender to the divine plan.

Complications arise when we try to control every element of a situation – even those where action is not required. It is very common for most of us (I am no exception to this) to think that it is our bounden duty to be the caretaker and controller of all the circumstances we endure. But that is not always the case. As I am penning down this chapter, I am reminded of an incident pertaining to my official work. I had a deadline that was fast approaching with regards to a task I had least knowledge about. I put in extra working hours to learn and gain sufficient knowledge about the task before actually getting started with it. I tried all possible means to get the work done along with my team members but some or the other issue kept cropping up. There were a number of dependencies on the way but we patiently marched ahead step by step. However, at one point everything just stopped abruptly and there seemed no way out .

I realized that my logical reasoning was leading me nowhere and everything was just shrouded in mystery. Actually, when confronted with contradictory ways during decision-making, it is best to let things loose and allow the job to happen. Allowing details to factor in by themselves helps greatly at times, as it lessens the resistance that we unwittingly add to the existing tense scene. I have seen wonders happen with me by just following this mantra with total faith. I know very well that it is not always possible to be in that zone of surrender and tranquility. But what if we are unable to spot a path to tread on? Do we want to wander endlessly and groan in pain? Surely not.

If we just keep following the breadcrumbs that are laid out for us without any preconceived notions and previous conditioning, events start to unfold with ease. Things start to reveal themselves spontaneously and steadily. There is clarity and everything falls into place perfectly at the right time. We then realize why certain events *had* to take place and we begin to soak ourselves in our new-found success. By taking a *leap of faith* into the unknown, we experience the flavor of ever-present magic in every speck of our life.

When the task got stuck, all of us felt hopeless. I had even stopped trying as I was too exhausted and mentally tired. However, my teammates continued working on it though intermittently with no results. I had almost decided to speak to my teammates about letting things be and even giving up at one point. Luckily, out of the blue, like a scene straight out of a movie our deadline was pushed forward by a few days. Now that the pressure had subsided a little, we began our brainstorming sessions once again with renewed vigor.

We started to explore newer perspectives that revealed the hidden problems which would have come up with the previous approach. By using a different and fresh method, the task was completed well within the second deadline. Later events proved that it was good that the first approach which we had chosen failed – it was a blessing in disguise for us. During the period where our ideas weren't succeeding and no track seemed to be visible, we kept ourselves busy by involving in other less demanding works. This gave room for alternatives to pop up to the physical realm by themselves and finally come into full blossom. This clearly teaches us that when we stop forcing things to happen and unfasten our control on a situation then a favorable outcome is assured.

Sometimes it becomes imperative for us to direct our thoughts deliberately in a different direction and make decisions accordingly. There may be times where we need to release the picture of what we thought and imagined our future would be like. Instead, we may have to make some hard decisions keeping in mind the happiness of everyone concerned. Trying to find satisfaction in the story we are actually in will help both our present and future to flourish. This may appear to be dogmatic and unrealistic. But acting based on the current need will take us a long way in our empowerment voyage.

Flowing joyously with a keen awareness to our vibrant setting will certainly take us ahead in our journey. Prioritizing our responsibilities and needs in the correct way will unquestionably sort out the numerous issues whirling in our minds. Paying gratitude to the countless favors that brighten our days will bring in more favorable events to us. A ten minute gratitude walk every day in nature can be very beneficial as it quiets our mind and stops all the useless chatter that bothers us all day long.

It is of utmost importance to create and maintain a balance not just for ourselves but also for our loved ones. We have heard people saying, 'Leave the past behind'. But is it that easy to pursue it? I am of the view that prolonged and dedicated effort is needed to bring in *this* mindset change. We need to figure out the lessons that we have learnt from our past instead of clinging on to the pain it has given us as we move forward boldly. Holding the lessons learnt close in our hearts is a sure shot way to improve one's life as it broadens our perspective. As we continue to calibrate and evaluate the knowledge gained meticulously, we get to experience countless benedictions in the form of our fulfilled desires. A well-deserved future can be a reality only if we are resilient enough to believe that it can come true for us.

CHAPTER SIX

RULES...RULES...RULES

The community we dwell in is bound by certain rules and regulations. This is mainly done for the safety and security of people so that every one of us can live fearlessly and peacefully. But how many of us adhere to the rules set by our elders and society? In other words, how many of us are willing to follow the guidelines that seem to serve as a protective shield? I am sure that many of us would have been snubbed at some point and forced to do things that ensure that we fit into the societal boundaries. And *every time* something like this happens, we push ourselves against the wall with no effect.

I am the youngest daughter of my parents and have been pampered by everyone in the family. From the time I can remember, I have *always* been told what to do. Whenever I was assigned a project at school, I was least worried as I knew that everything would be taken care of for me. My sisters took it upon themselves to plan every single detail required for the project and worked tirelessly to get *my* project done on time. I was a spectator and a bystander while everything was being done for me. I enjoyed the special treatment being given to me and considered myself extremely fortunate. The cushioning and concern in the initial years were immensely overpowering.

It felt great to be protected and safe. But as time passed by, I noticed and observed that I was seeking validation for every act of mine. My decision-making ability was both biased as well as eclipsed. I was influenced by what my mind was impregnated with from my childhood. If I was questioned as to why I had followed a specific plan for my project, similar to a parrot, I could only tell my teachers that part which was explained to me by my sisters. However, if ever another approach was delineated for the same project, my mind would go blank. I used to feel embarrassed and get into freeze mode. The reason for this was quite simple and straightforward. I had no idea or knowledge about the intricate details of the project as the work was entirely carried out by my sisters.

I could barely think through the facts correctly and make decisions on my own. I basically didn't have the confidence in myself and my capabilities. I believed that my ideas were not good enough and bound to fail. I couldn't gather the courage to put my proposal into operation for the fear of failure. It took years for me to realize that all this was my illusion and a result of my low self-concept. This made me quite restless and grumpy. It is an eternal truth that our society is conditioned in such a way that friends and relatives play a major role in building an individual's perception of life.

Once this realization occurred, I wanted to have control over the situation and take responsibility for my actions. I decided that I wanted to put my brain to work and reap its benefits rather than being a mere onlooker. I wanted to fix everything around me with immediate effect. Working on my schoolwork and projects topped the list. I started with researching and learning concepts well in advance before getting started with any project that was allotted to me. Once this was done, I came up with a step by step plan that could be put into the works. All this while no one at home knew about the preparations I was engaged in. I wanted to amaze everyone at home with my work and hence decided to keep it confidential until its completion.

I was very excited to share my findings with my sisters even before presenting them at school. I wanted to surprise them with my answers. But to my dismay, even before I could show them my solution, they had everything worked out perfectly for me. I was dumbstruck and shell-shocked. I didn't want to upset them as they had invested their valuable time for me. I went ahead and presented their work at school but was extremely sad from within.

I made sure no at home knew about this as I didn't want to bother anyone with my new-found mindset. I felt that I was not able to get out of the rut I had gotten myself into. The more I tried to free myself and resist it, the more I was disappointed. I could find no way out of my plight and seriously did not know what actions to take. I started condemning the old beliefs as I found it complicated to accept them. The above incident that I have mentioned may look like any other normal situation that we regularly face. But I am of the view that we are never able to guess which episode can turn our entire life around in a split second.

It was *this* incident that had a deep impact on me and worked extensively on my psyche. After prolonged thinking, I came to the conclusion that had I told my sisters the surprise that was in store for them at first place, my work would have found its way to the presentation. I was determined to take initiative and speak up whenever a situation demanded. With an over-enthusiastic attitude, I set about on my secret mission of being proactive. I started to delve deeper into every subject of my interest so that I could decode the plot.

Unfortunately, my *unanswerable* questions were met with severe backlash from everyone, and this further compounded my wounds. They were interpreted as my negligence to revere elders in the family, and eventually, I was silenced. I questioned myself several times if it was worth walking on this path? I literally felt very bad for my parents as they got embarrassed many a times for my deeds. I felt very guilty for my actions. Therefore, I cautiously restrained myself from getting into any discussions on controversial subjects.

This is a scenario that many of US are familiar with. I would also like to point out that there are also a *special few* who wholeheartedly accept and are happy with no regret. No offence is made to such people in this book. I strongly opine that these people should be appreciated for their perseverance and tenacity. I am entirely against the idea of disrespecting our elders in order to accomplish our motives. I believe that taking decisions irrationally and, on an impulse, will not be of any help to us. It not just causes friction in our relationships but also puts us in a dilemma.

If there is no proper planning and forethought from our end, then we are bound to mess things up. Undoubtedly, all through my life I have always respected my elders and valued their opinions highly by incorporating them efficiently in my life. At the same time, I have also encountered occasions in my life where I have had to take tough decisions depending on the need of the moment. Always keeping our loved ones informed about our actions and seeking their guidance whenever required strengthens the relationship bond.

If we make the effort to develop the habit of listening, it can reduce the awkwardness present among the family members to a large extent. Keeping communications crisp and transparent can help both the parties involved to a great extent. We, more often than not, listen to a conversation so that we can speak and put forward our opinions. Being a parent has taught me the importance and need to work on our listening skills. I never knew about it until one fine day my daughter brought it to my notice.

Like every other kid, my daughter talks continuously about every possible matter that she is allowed to and there is no end to it. Most of the times I am busy completing other menial tasks that are common in every household during our conversations. There are even times when I hardly listen to her and just keep nodding my head in agreement. Like any other day, we were busy talking about her friends. She had actually planned a playdate with her friends and wanted my permission for it. She was busy finding ways to convince me and promised to complete all her schoolwork well in time. It seemed as if I was listening to her, but I was in my own world planning my schedule for the next day. Like always I nodded my head in approval without my knowledge and we went ahead with our day.

I was very surprised at her unusual behavior the next day when she finished all her work even before I could remind her. I never realized that she was eagerly looking forward to her playdate until she told me. The problem was, we had other plans worked out for that same evening. The moment I realized my folly, I felt abashed and remorseful for failing her. Though we later rescheduled our plans, and the matter was sorted I learnt the need to keep our ears fully open.

Only when we carefully listen to what others are speaking, can we grasp the situation at hand. Luckily for me, we could re-schedule our plans and I could handle the commotion easily. But what about situations that are vital and hold great importance where there is no room for negligence. We should be a good listener so that we can understand the underlying problem at hand and be in a position to offer a plausible solution when asked for.

I have always wanted to set myself free from the chains set by our society and frame my own agenda. However, setting oneself free from the age-old philosophies doesn't mean that we end up causing furor and imbalance everywhere. If our opinions and decisions cause more harm than benefit, I suggest that we should re-evaluate our options. Whenever I realized that my decisions were impacting me and my family negatively, I have taken account of the situation at an early stage. By aligning my moves in the best interests of everyone concerned and making the appropriate changes have always worked to my advantage.

It may look as if I am contradicting my own views. However, that is not the case because all of us love and care for our dear ones. We would not want to hurt them on purpose and weaken our relationships. To be honest, I have taken some drastic steps that left me with no retreat.I had severed all ties and now, filling the void seems nearly impossible. I have learnt the hard way that in most cases it is best to make strategic and well-planned moves that are beneficial to one and all.

I know for sure that rule-breakers are not very welcome in our society as a result of my first-hand experience in the matter. Nevertheless, by giving them the benefit of doubt and talking calmly, we simplify things in our society. I don't mean to single out anyone nor do I wish to encourage any particular group. On the other hand, I always presume that every one of us is a part of society and has a moral responsibility towards it. It becomes a lot easier when every one of us is open to trying new ideas and is willing to be flexible. To avoid repeating history, I now ensure that as a parent I give my daughter the necessary space so that she can explore her creative side all by herself. Unless she seeks our help and doesn't make the first move, we refrain from entering the scene. At home, we always encourage her to speak up even if she is hesitant and insist her to put down her ideas on paper. By doing this not only do we understand her line of thought but also know when to direct her (only provided the situation demands).

All of us will agree with me that none of us would want to put our loved ones and friends in humiliating situations. It pains a lot to see our parents and elders facing the heat for our actions. Such testing and tough times fill us with nothing but guilt and remorse. I regret some of my decisions taken on the spur of the moment, for which my parents and elders had to pay the price. At this juncture, I wish to discuss one such incident that is still afresh in my mind and reminds me to be watchful of my actions.

There was this particular wedding which we were supposed to attend when I was in high school. Everyone at home was very excited to be travelling for the wedding. However, I was the least interested of all to attend the ceremony due to my limiting beliefs and apprehensions about mingling with everyone due to my introvert nature as already stated in Chapter 4 - Acceptance of Oneself. Though everything was going perfectly at the wedding , I felt out of place and was only looking forward to getting back to my nest – our home. I was very happy as the festivities ended when all of a sudden, a slight disagreement erupted between my cousins and my sister. My sister was derided during the course of the altercation that upset all of us. I felt that it was unfair that she was singled out by all the other cousins and cornered. I couldn't hold myself back and spoke in favor of her. After that all hell broke loose, and until today we have not been able to get things back to normal. My parents were reprimanded for my actions, and I stood there writhing in pain over the misery which they had to suffer due to me.

Moving ahead optimistically has been quite difficult but getting over the past by learning from my experiences has benefitted me notably.

"The only source of knowledge is Experience." - Albert Einstein

I am eager to share the lessons that I have learnt in my journey so far with everyone. It is very natural for each and every one of us to find ourselves in the midst of confusion and temporary failure as we progress in our lives. Proper assessment of situations, keeping in mind all their pros and cons, will definitely help us find the balance that we are seeking. Thoughtless and irrational actions taken in a desperate move to prove ourselves to the society are sure to fail. They not only bring in unnecessary turmoil but also wreak havoc everywhere.

Calling the shots in a state of impatience is mostly based on the emotions of fear and insecurity. The need for validation is normally an act that stems out of low self-confidence. All of us know that all the ill-feeling, negative thoughts that veil our minds temporarily, make us powerless. We are aware that inciting such pessimistic emotions within us puts us totally off the path. We need to train ourselves to make our choices keeping in mind the opinions of people concerned. Consequently, our gains and rewards will be in huge proportions. By being consciously aware of our actions and their effects on everyone concerned about us, we make significant progress along the way in every domain.

CHAPTER SEVEN

SELF-IMAGE

All of us are an integral part of society and world at large. The way the fraternity and the people in our inner circle perceive us is given lots of importance. Therefore, it is essential that we pay considerable attention to the way we carry ourselves in public. It becomes imperative that we create an image of ourselves that draws more brownie points for us. Self-image plays a major role in our personal growth as it allows us to advertise ourselves *in the way we wish* to the world. By portraying ourselves as a confident and outgoing personality, it becomes easy to socialize and make friends. However, steady effort needs to be put in order to maintain the image created. Networking for the purposes of career or business can be done with greater efficiency and smoothness through this makeover.

Every human being on this planet, with no exceptions made, wishes to be liked and appreciated by others. It is very inherent for every individual to feel in such a way as pleasing and affectionate words boosts our self-confidence in a major way. By admiring and cheering we can motivate and increase the efficiency of the workers. For example, a small act of appreciation on the part of an employer fires up the employees to a large extent. The creativity levels raises and the passion of the staff towards work increases as well. The employees in the team get inspired to perform better than before.

"A strong, positive self-image is the best possible preparation for success." – Joyce Brothers

Out of the box ideas that help to grow the business are easily delivered by eager and enthusiastic employees. Constant reminders about deadlines and policing may not at all be needed. Whenever our work is applauded, we get the impression that our hard work is being recognized by the higher authorities. For those of us who are in the race to prove our worth, the acclaim coming our way serves as a trigger that help boost our careers. On the contrary, if we are criticized it impacts us to a great extent and lowers our self-confidence. We get the feeling that all our efforts have gone down the drain and consequently our excitement towards work diminishes. We no longer show the interest to get involved or participate in office activities. That in turn affects our performance and the cycle continues. We get entangled in a dead-lock situation from which there is no way out.

All of us must have had cousins, friends or colleagues who are quite popular in our community. They are the center of attraction in every social gathering that they attend and are the cynosure of all eyes. Such people are always in the limelight wherever they go. I have also been in such situations as I was growing up and I always wondered how come everyone is smitten by *this* one person's charisma. It felt enigmatic and I was very curious to know how to embody that type of personality. The praises and compliments constantly showered on that person were the icing on the cake.

Everything seemed so surreal, and I imagined myself being the central character of my movie. I had a cousin whose charm and aura mesmerized one and all. I was so drawn to her magnetic personality that I secretly wished I could become like her. Seeing her being extolled and treated *specially* for her persona by everybody further fueled my wish. I just loved *that* feeling of adulation. I just had only one thought in mind all day long – to be popular and have many friends. I have already mentioned at the beginning of the book that I was a shy and timid kid. Yet, the idea of being famous was so strong and thrilling that I failed to realize that it was in complete contrast to my nature.

I was not ready to settle for anything less and refused to accept the truth. I imagined being doted on by everyone for my transformation. I was in my own world daydreaming and fantasizing about how wonderful everything is going to turn out. I thought that it was going to be a cake walk for me and doing it would be fun. I had never done or even tried to do something like that before, but I was so fascinated with the idea that I wanted to venture into this adventure at any cost. My mind was totally preoccupied with thoughts of laughter and joy without thinking even once about the consequences (if things failed).

I learnt about the concept of self-image by carefully and keenly making mental notes of how people were treated by society. I was already aware of self-image and the effect it has on the psychology of a person. This meant that self-image as an abstract idea was compelling and had a profound influence on an individual's intellect. With the knowledge I had gained from my own research, I went about trying to alter my already existing image. I kept it as a top notch secret and didn't share my game plan with anyone, not even my sisters.

I tried to do stuff that put me in lots of embarrassing and tricky situations. I tried to mimic the way my cousin dressed and behaved. It felt very weird, but the pie was so enticing that it pushed me to give my best shot. My mom and sisters thought that something was wrong with me and kept checking on me constantly. But not once did I reveal my undercover mission to them. Though it was quite cumbersome, I continued relentlessly. I was busy trying to impress everyone by engaging in activities that were unlike mine.

In my quest of being liked by everyone, unknowingly I developed a sense of envy and jealousy towards people I was trying to emulate. I either ignored my cousin whenever I met her or kept myself away from going to parties. Whenever I was questioned by my parents for my unusual behavior, I gave them reasons that were completely absurd and irrelevant. The reason for this was quite strange - I didn't know what was happening with me and why I was behaving in a different manner? I realized this much later when I started introspecting my qualities.

When I analyzed my moves after many years, it became very clear that I was finding ways to avoid meeting my cousin and hence stopped going to get-togethers. I was very much displeased with myself for falling short of my expectations. Seeing my cousin would add salt to my fresh wounds and remind me of my failure. Despite investing a lot of time and energy on this activity, I wasn't happy at all. The results weren't encouraging, and I was far behind the expected target. This left me annoyed and vexed. I became impulsive and irritable.

I felt that I was not being true to myself and did not know where I was going wrong. By forcefully indulging in acts that finally disappointed me, I felt stuck in a cage. As I had not spoken about this to my sisters and mom, I thought that I couldn't approach them for help either. I feared being admonished and rebuked by them for my foolish actions. I was like a cat on the wall not knowing what to do. The reality was, neither did I succeed in my image-building task, nor did I own up to my original individuality.

"The greatest thing that you can give yourself is freedom from what others think." - Abraham Hicks

There is no doubt that by building the *right* self-image, we ensure that our evolution speeds up owing to the fact that the emotions of self-doubt get vanquished. Depressing and cynical thoughts no longer exist. A new sense of confidence and self-assuredness sprouts up within us that brings about a positive change in our personality. A wave of optimism and hopefulness constantly buoys us into newer heights. Subsequently, success is guaranteed in every sphere that definitely encourages us further. Undoubtedly, it is the right self-image that does all the magic of leveling up and upgrading a person's Life in the right direction.

More often than not, it is noticed that there is a mismatch between our original personality and the one we are trying to ape. The image we portray and the role we had enjoyed enacting so far begins to stifle us. A person who was always in high spirits appears lost and dull. This is exactly what I went through. When I tried getting involved in pursuits that were not something that I normally would engage in, I started messing things up. I was someone who hardly spoke in a gathering and now I began to strike a conversation out of the blue. Though I used to initiate the conversation, I couldn't get myself to speak properly and confidently. I worked a lot on myself to get into the groove and never gave up even once.

Nevertheless, as time went by, I got tired of all the drama and just wanted to put an end to it. This is one of the many incidents in our lives where a miscalculation from our end pushes us into troubled waters. We start to feel stuck, anxious and uncomfortable in our self-created film. But the most frequent questions to ask ourselves are – what went wrong and how do we free ourselves from the self-deceptive move? Contemplation and self-analysis can alleviate our mental conflict substantially.

It is quite common to imbibe certain qualities which may not be a part of our nature, to be in the spotlight. We sometimes wish to captivate everyone by our actions, which is totally understandable. It is not wrong to act in certain ways so that we will be credited by everyone around us. But what most of us do not realize is that we take on the role of a *people-pleaser* in the guise of revamping our self-image. We do this due to lack of proper self-analysis and self-reflection. We do not study the odds that are stacked against us and end up in a soup. By not weighing our options properly, we end up walking on the edge of a razor.

People-pleasing is a herd-mentality that is prevalent from ages across all strata of society. It eases our path and gives us a direct entry into the core group that is highly influential. It assists us in fitting into the boundaries set by the community safely and quickly. Sycophancy aids us in being favored wherever we go on account of our closeness to the core people. By this can get our work done in a jiffy and hardly make any effort in doing hard work. However, there is a fine line and a minute difference between being a people-pleaser and the basic idea of self-image.

I do not say that people-pleasers are right or wrong – it is completely an individual's choice. I am not here to call anyone out as every view outlined in this book is entirely from my standpoint. I do not wish to hurt or belittle anyone as every one of us is sensible enough to make our own choices. In reality, I believe that this is an exceptional skill to be able to do this when in fact we do not possess the said qualities. I am of the opinion that being a people-pleaser is not everyone's cup of tea and is quite strenuous. When we put on the garb of a person with whom we are not able to relate to, we are essentially trying to impress people. It is actually a very delicate situation to be in.

"A true self-image will be based on how much you are living out your values." – Steve Peters

In keeping up with the wrong self-developed image, we bring about needless concerns and worries that are totally uncalled for. It becomes an arduous task, and we get exhausted in doing so. There are so many pent up emotions that make way for irritation and temper issues. Though I started my motive with just altering and redoing my image, I never realized when I started to put on a façade. Only when things got out of control did it dawn on me. In such cases, our intuition is our best friend whom we can trust blindly (Chapter 4 - Acceptance of Oneself). Our emotions warn and guide us right in time and it is up to us to be watchful.

When I noticed that I was exhausted all day long despite no excess physical work and stopped enjoying the activity of remodeling, I decided it was high time I take ownership of the situation. My gut feeling indicated that trouble was round the corner and only then did I realize my mistake. Similarly, every one of us may be in a state where we find it odd and frightening to speak out about our deep-seated fears. The notion of being harshly treated and mocked prevents us from taking any productive action.

We are lost in our own discerning impressions about ourselves. It may look as if it is a dead ender, and we are doomed forever.

Moreover, when we are into the right self-image makeover, we are trying to improve and better ourselves. We are looking at uplifting ourselves that enhances our quality of Life. Our mind overflows with progressive views about various aspects that need our attention, and we begin to inspire everyone around us. By identifying our strengths and weaknesses, we know exactly what steps need to be taken to elevate ourselves. We advance both materialistically as well as spiritually. When we take pertinent actions, we obtain huge results in the form of wide-spread acclaim and accolades. As long as we keep ourselves from overdoing or from crossing the fine line and getting entangled in an unwanted mess, we are bound to benefit from the right changeover. Constant practice of meticulously observing our environment to assimilate the right qualities is of immense benefit in our advancement towards self-discovery.

CHAPTER EIGHT

SELF-IMAGE VS OUR RULES

It is rare that we come across people who say that they do not care what the world says about them. Such people stand by their actions and live based on their own principles. They do not bother much about the price that they will have to pay for this. Everyone else's opinions just fall on deaf ears. Such people are least interested in impressing others and/or being in their good books. These people are mostly absorbed within themselves and live life on their own terms. They feel that *everyone* is against them, trying to pull them down and constantly criticizing them.

However, we do have a majority of people in the world who are quite clear about their thoughts and seek a vent to speak up. These people wish to have a say in specific matters but fail to put their words into action. The reason for this is their deep-rooted fear of being rejected and detested by their loved ones. They do have certain strong notions about specific concepts but choose to keep mum. Due to their inability to articulate their views effectively, they prefer to keep their suggestions to themselves. They assume that their friends and family members might despise their ideas or deride them.

We have already seen that self-image plays a vital role in defining the way society views us. The way we are treated in social gatherings is directly influenced by our image in public. The reason for this is that people identify us only by the image that we have projected to the world . Society assumes this image to be true and confirms it to be the actual personality of the individual. People in a community are able to identify us *only* with this image and cannot relate to anything other than this. In general, it is human tendency that we normally do not wish to look beyond what is served to us.

Conclusions are drawn based on what most of the masses believe to be real or what is visible.

The concept of self-image is like a double-edged sword that needs to be handled with utmost care. It is like walking on a tightrope where every step needs to be taken strategically. All of us know that what we sow is what we can expect to reap as our fruit. Hence a wrong move on our part can put us in tough and grueling situations that may take years to get fixed. I would like to reprise the agony I was going through in keeping up with *my popular image* and how it took a toll on my mental health as discussed in Chapter 7 - Self-Image. I found myself trying very hard to come out of it as at one point it started choking me and made things very cumbersome for me. In some cases, even this may not be possible, and we end up bearing the brunt for our entire life. We may find ourselves bonded and restrained, not able to get away from all the jazz that is going on around us.

We have discussed at length in Chapter 6 - Rules...Rules...Rules how some persons like to set their own rules and are not willing to accept what the society has in store for them. Such people are comfortable in their own skin and wish to be the trendsetters. They defy all odds and hesitate to fit themselves into the boundaries set by society. Sometimes, or should I say most of the times, they may seem to be uncooperative, and it is only with great difficulty that they may be convinced. It takes significant effort on the part of the family members to get things done easily without any complications and needless discussions.

At first sight, such people may seem to be *troublemakers* who want to have a say in every matter and cause ruckus everywhere they go. In a like manner, my moves were mostly perceived to be irksome and also unnecessary by many in my social circle. It seemed to everyone that I was doing all this only to be in the limelight and gain prominence. None really took the effort or pain to understand the actual reason behind my deeds. I also agree to the fact that no one in this world really has the time for it. I suppose that it is easier to pass judgements for everyone than investing time in analyzing others.

It may appear that the so-called troublemakers question every move made by the family members as it is their in-born nature. But a mature observation and proper scrutiny can help us understand the latent frustration hidden within them. The only way to handle such people is to carefully analyze their behavior and look for incidents that might have deeply affected them. I strongly opine that when we try to dive deep into the issue instead of reprimanding the troublemakers, the actual reasons come to light.

I presume that all of us are shaped by the limitless experiences that we come across in our daily lives. An unusual mannerism of a person that is strikingly apart from the crowd should strike a note in our minds and push us to dig in further. When we attempt to really understand someone, we may come across certain facts related to them that may even shock us. This reminds me of one of my friends who was caught in a similar situation. I had a friend who was considered arrogant and brash by everyone. Initially even I had the same perception about her. Nevertheless, her nature made me curious and as time passed, I realized the real reason for her aggressive nature - an unhealed wound of her past that she was clinging onto similar to me. At such times, self-love plays a pivotal role as it opens our eyes to a wider and accepting world. It fills us with empathy and compassion towards our fellow beings.

We have seen that a self-image that is faked to attract attention from people is a canker to the soul. It does no good to us other than messing up our life. It may give us momentary pleasure but at one point it may become a burden that is too heavy to carry. By creating a beautiful image that we may not be able to resonate with, we are sure to invite problems for ourselves. We may find ourselves caged and stuck with no scope of withdrawal. Pulling through it and living in the self-initiated delusion may become a herculean task. Over a period of time, acknowledging it may no longer be possible for us.

There may be times when our self-image and our opinions do not match. Such situations normally arise when we have strong opinions and are not willing to budge. It is at such times that we do not get influenced easily and believe in holding our stand. We are clear about our preferences and choices. It is then that we mince no words in letting people know about it and keep ourselves away from faking. Most of the time, we may even be at loggerheads with even our closest friends and do not mind getting involved in heated arguments.

What exactly happens when our self-image and our opinions have a tug-of-war? This situation is pretty interesting and worth discussing because both of them are about the same person. These are different facets to the same individual's personality. Self-image is in itself a notion where we take up a role that helps us garner compliments and adulation. We assume *this* personality unknowingly right from our childhood because it enthralls us and piques our interest. As we start enacting that role, we gradually try to embody that person (as seen in most cases). It becomes more of an obligation to stand true to that role.

As long as the image we try to depict does not harm us in any way, it is perfectly fine. If we enjoy our role play and also benefit extensively from it, then there is nothing like it. This is a sign that we are on the right path to self-development. We begin to assimilate *those extra* qualities that will aid us greatly in the future. I am in favor of the fact that the *right* self-image greatly motivates and empowers us to confidently present ourselves before everyone. I suppose that any action taken on our part that affects us mentally should be accounted for at the earliest.

Opinions play a significant role in developing us as a person. They bring out the actual personality of an individual. When effectively put in words, the viewpoints that we put forth before everyone help us immensely as they let the entire world know about our thoughts. It is vital that we speak the right words at the right time, and to the right audience. Else they lose their worth and we land ourselves in a tight spot. Most of us have heard our elders recommending us to think and let out our words before speaking. Once we think and speak cautiously, we avoid blurting out uneasy words that not just hurt our ears but also wound our soul. Words are like arrows that cannot be taken back once they are let out. It is hundred percent true that by following this principle, we prevent unpleasant situations.

Opinionated people seek clarity and certainty while taking actions. They mostly prefer to keep themselves away from reckless and superfluous talk. They do not talk in the air and look for credibility in people. They are coherent and carefully weigh their words. This nature of putting forth their opinions fearlessly in public and sticking to their own ideas, makes it easy for us to identify them. We can spot such people effortlessly as they stand out in the group. Image-making is an exercise that happens over an entire life span starting right from our childhood. It is not a one-time activity and there is no such thing as being done with it. Consistently refining and making the required changes gives us excellent results.

When one tries to fill a plate that is already overflowing, it is then that hitches arise. What does this sentence mean? Let us delve further into this aspect by taking the case of a fictitious character – person X. X has always wanted to have a large circle of friends and likes to mingle with everyone. He has observed that to have many friends, he will need to make substantial changes in his persona, so as to get into the groove. He realizes that in order to be accepted by his friends he will have to put in lots of effort to be liked by them.

So, he takes great pains and finally becomes the star attraction of his friend's group. X is a person who is very clear about his decisions and likes to abide by certain principles. But for the sake of his friends and to be one among them, he tries to overlook these minor issues initially. However, as days progress, he finds himself in a fix. He feels cornered and is in a dilemma as to what exactly went wrong? Likewise, when we encounter such predicament in our lives what measures should we take to prevent it from affecting our future?

When the two dimensions to a personality are contradictory in nature, it becomes a strenuous and exhausting task to continuously maintain them. It is similar to the case of riding two boats at the same time and not having control of any of them. This way we are sure to meet with accidents and end up in a mishap. This is one of the main reasons why personality development is very crucial in today's times. Molding the traits of a person is an ongoing process and a systematic approach is highly desirable to build it. Hence it is absolutely essential to maintain a fine balance between image-building and setting the right priorities so that it ensures a smooth ride.

CHAPTER NINE

The Power of Now

It is commonplace in every household for parents and children to have conversations regarding the child's future plans. When I was a child, I *actually* wanted to grow up fast and get into college. Once I was in college, I wanted to finish my studies quickly and start earning. I was under the impression that by pursuing a job, I would gain freedom and independence. I assumed that I could live on my own terms without being accountable to anyone at home. I thought that I could make my own decisions, and no one at home would question me. This series of events is typical for every one of us, and I suppose that it is relatable.

I am of the opinion that most of the readers must have thought in the same way as I did because as human beings, we always like to dream about our future. We want to figure out our entire path right now, *at this very moment*. The truth is that we are never completely happy or fulfilled in our present moment. We always have an irking feeling at the back of our minds that never lets us rest in peace. It is this restlessness that does not allow us to enjoy our victories wholeheartedly. Predominantly, we fail to realize that our likes, interests and preferences keep changing every split second. In addition to this, all of us know the vital role that family, friends and society play in shaping our mindset.

In our schooling days, most of us do not find anything interesting or worthwhile other than spending time with our friends. We find our hands tied up and mostly show less interest in academics. We like to get involved in extracurricular activities and games as it gives us a chance to make friends. We wish to grow up as soon as possible. We long to take up a job as the *very* thought of independence seems fresh and exciting. The income that comes in line with it is the icing on the cake that entices us. But how many of us enjoy the initial feeling of exhilaration which we expect from our new employment? How long do we persist in the feeling of freedom that we were eagerly anticipating?

I remember eagerly awaiting and even planning the outfits for my first job. I was so excited for my first job that I had butterflies in my stomach and could not sleep the previous night. Sadly, a few days into the job I found myself feeling low most of the times for reasons I could not decipher. I was totally lost and felt stranded. I began to lose focus in my work and consequently my performance declined. I was totally confused at my absurd behavior as this was *the* job that I was looking forward to joining. I questioned myself several times about my present state of mind and if I had made a wrong decision regarding the job. Unfortunately, I had no answers to it.

"The primary cause of unhappiness is never the situation but your thoughts about it." - Eckhart Tolle

I hope that all of us will surely agree to the fact that we are always on the run, in the chase of that one element or shall I say, ***'the X factor'*** . We are forever on the lookout for answers to our endless queries. We are desperately searching for the missing piece in the hope of completing the puzzle in which we find ourselves. We seem to feel incomplete and astray. We have a lingering feeling similar to the one when we misplace a piece of exquisite jewelry that is normally kept safe. Though our intuition (Chapter 4 – Acceptance of Oneself) reminds us through our low-vibration emotions that things are slipping out of our control, we fail to listen to it and take the required action.

I was dull all through the day and just wanted to be in the bed doing nothing at all. I definitely knew that I was wasting my precious time but did not know the cause for my lack of interest in any work. There are many such incidents that may at first glance seem like a mystery and that there is no way out for us. We are unable to comprehend the situation at hand and don't know whom to ask for advice. In a state of despair, we begin to knock on every other door that pops up in front of us.

Most of the us find ourselves in utter confusion with no sense of direction. We are clueless about our mood swings which are so quirky. With no proper anchor, we are sure to meet with accidents or mishaps. Doesn't this seem familiar and also surprisingly shocking? I am sure all of us would want to know why something like this happens in the first place. Another question that comes up is, can we avert such situations and do something about them? Without further ado, let us get into the finer details and learn about them.

We need to always keep in mind that setting expectations that are closer to reality helps us greatly in every arena – be it personal and professional. It is very good to think about times ahead as it helps us to take proper actions and make well-thought decisions. However, wanting and trying to incessantly live in the future causes havoc. In most cases, we get so engrossed and deeply involved in the forthcoming periods that we completely forget the actual key to our bliss. The answer is right in our hands.

"Life is always in motion, so you cannot be stuck." - Abraham Hicks

It is crucial for us to time and again remind ourselves that Life is irreversible. The instant that is experienced once can only be cherished in our memories. We can in no way go back in time. We need to know the worth of the ***one golden moment*** that we have with us right here, right now – the present moment. The moment that is of utmost importance and is like flowing water. Just as we cannot touch the water that has passed by, in the same way we cannot go back to that specific period. When we constantly try to fast-forward our sojourn, we fail to make the required adjustments and assess our prospects correctly.

"The past has no power over the present moment." - Eckhart Tolle

It is only in the *now* that we can create both beautiful memories as well as marvelous wonders. Those beautiful memories can definitely be revisited later by us, especially in our low moments to remind us of how wonderful everything around us has been all this while. These wonderful, uplifting moments keep us fired up to continue our travel with hope and expectancy. But unconsciously, we get our past into the present by either talking about them frequently or keeping them alive in our minds. In doing so, we forget that the past is already gone and also, we eventually spoil the best time as well - our glorious present that is right before us.

It is rightly said that we are the creators of our own reality. It is our thoughts that make us the person we claim to be. By thinking wisely and being aware of our thought patterns, it is possible to bring a huge difference in our habitat. Honestly, we spend most of our time either regretting our past events or praying for a better future. What does this statement imply? It means that we are hardly experiencing the emotions of the most powerful moment at hand. It is not wrong to think about our past or plan for the rainy days as long as we do not allow them to sabotage and overshadow our present.

"Your life is right now." - Esther Hicks

Constant juggling between the past and subsequent times does no good to us. It just increases our anxiety levels and causes unwanted stress. The reason for this is that we don't have our feet firmly grounded at one place. In reality, we are all over the place finding ways to fix all our problems right at *this* point of time. Though physically I was working in my dream job and going to the office daily, my mind was preoccupied and aimlessly seeking for something more – the unknown. I couldn't gauge my feelings properly and didn't know what I was searching endlessly. To the outside world, everything seemed perfect, but I felt something amiss.

All of us need to keep in mind that we are on the exterior just a body of matter. But in its entirety, there is much more to it than what is visible to us. At this point, I wish to reiterate that we are the substance of all our previous conditioning and experiences put together as a whole. Our thoughts and actions are interrelated and build our individuality. Our activities are almost always influenced by the events we run into day in and day out. Indisputably, I would like to say that we are spoilt by choice and always choose to complicate our atmosphere.

I learnt from my experience that I was mindlessly looking for a job, *but* not the right job in my field of interest. It was much later that I realized this truth, but by then the damage had already been done. I had wasted years in useless complaining and fretting that proved futile. All my attempts to succeed were counterproductive and ineffective. I criticized myself for not living up to my expectations let alone my parents' hopes from me. If I had taken a moment to introspect my interests and choices, I would have been spared the pain of dejection and self-pity.

We do the same with our upcoming days as well. By this I mean that we love to bring the forthcoming events into our present. We love to think and draw plans for an enriching future but to what extent this would work in our best interests is a question that needs sound evaluation. What does 'would work' in our best interests' signify? Whenever we talk about our plans, we are most likely to be in high spirits and pure joy at the very thought of those desires. But as we continue with our conversations or thoughts, unintentionally those feelings are slowly but for sure replaced by emotions of self-doubt and fear as seen in most cases.

At this point, let us take a moment to introspect our thoughts to the best of our knowledge in order to comprehend ourselves better. I know for a fact that most of us, if not all, experience a rise and fall of emotions. It is but generic and there is no cause for worry or discontent. What exactly is happening in these cases? Let us try to explore the events piece by piece. We start off on a very high note and are very excited about our aspirations. As we sustain these thoughts of enthusiasm and effervescence for a longer period of time, we acquire huge advantages from them, because these high-vibe emotions stimulate our actions making our road to success much easier.

I was super excited to be taking up the first job of my career and the idea of financial freedom added to my excitement. However, along the way the very job that was the driving force behind my enthusiasm slowly began to lose its steam as I had not weighed in the odds properly. As previously mentioned, I was so much into self-criticism that I failed to look for solutions to fix the issues. When we let our emotions be superseded by angst and apprehensions, neither can we expect a bright future nor a peaceful present. We live in distress and self-inflicted abuses that disturb our current time in a great way.

Does this mean that we should not be working on planning a bountiful yield? Surely not, because we do need a certain amount of brainstorming and meaningful discussions in order to ensure a bright produce. As long as scouting for better possibilities is not overpowering and putting our present at stake, it is perfectly fine to continue to do so. We need to know where to draw the line so that our future does not control our present. There is a minor difference between driving our present and controlling our present. Dwelling into this aspect a little more and taking a moment to assimilate its spirit proves to be very fruitful and beneficial.

Most of the time, because of our self-expectations we get so enamored and obsessed with certain ideas that we do not realize the negative effect they have on us holistically. *Those certain ideas* begin to ghost our present and control it. We miss out on details that are affecting our day-to-day routine and swiftly everything in our ecosystem starts to go downhill filling it with murky, black clouds.

The phrase 'control' by definition means dominating. It gives us a sense of taking over and plays with our emotions. We find our expectations failing and not being fulfilled. Unlike this, the chief idea of 'drive' is totally contrasting from the word 'control'.

I have no doubt that the word 'drive' evokes a sense of optimism and confidence in the mind of everyone reading the book at this moment. This is exactly the point I was trying to explain and reason out. When the conversations about our dreams have more to do with constructive planning and a strong, unshakeable belief in ourselves, then we are headed in the right direction. It appears at first instance that it is just a trivial matter, and it is not a big deal. However, on mature thought, we realize that it is actually an important and powerful mindset shift that is desired to garner the gifts that are in store for us.

"The journey of a thousand miles begins with one step." - Lao Tzu

When every single thing around us seems to be crumbling and all our plans of action come crashing down, it leaves us in a state of total dissatisfaction. It is in such scenarios that we need to identify the red flags flying high on our path and take immediate charge of the situation. It is very important that we acknowledge the *now* and take actions based on what is occurring in the given moment because, by doing this, we can be sure that the upcoming events will be in accordance with our visions. It becomes easy to push ourselves in the direction of our desired prospects when we begin to soak ourselves completely in one moment at a time.

'Live in the Present' is the sole mantra that we need to assimilate in our life. It is vital that we practice it religiously and soak up in its spirit so that we can be confident of a bountiful harvest ahead. We are guaranteed immeasurable success and fortune once we understand how powerful our *now* is. There is no doubt that we will be filled with ever-increasing growth and richness once we begin to absorb the true essence of this mantra. As children, we have been taught in school that the fruits of our hard work are always sweet. This is an undeniable principle that appropriately fits in these circumstances. A little effort on our part to be well-aware of our thoughts pays great dividends.

Can we relive our painful experiences of the past from a different stance that could help us receive exorbitant gains? Likewise, some ideas that we perceive with unto belief as problems in our tomorrow are nothing but a mere hallucination of our minds. How do we cross this bridge of our confused emotions that are constantly weighing us down and tripping our balance? I would like to remind all the readers about the hidden power that we have been equipped with – the tool of freewill (Chapter 3 - Concept of Freewill). It is at this juncture that we can use our faculty of freewill ably and efficiently.

Regardless of what we encounter in the present instant, if we remain composed and refrain from giving knee-jerk reactions, there is definitely a scope for gradual improvement in our conditions. It is typical of us to get caught up in either our past or our future intermittently, especially when the present situations pan out somewhat differently and are not as per our expectations. It is then that we need to catch hold of the hostile thoughts immediately and pivot them in the direction of better, refreshing thoughts. Pivoting is mindfully and consciously routing our thoughts in a positive way, so that we feel good about ourselves. If our past is haunting us, then shutting it off abruptly (which is next to possible) is not going to serve us in any way, because the more we resist it, the more it resurfaces based on the law of action and reaction.

A better approach would be to distract ourselves for the time being from those bitter episodes and pull back our minds to our present. Focusing on our previous achievements and patting ourselves on the back for how far we have come despite the challenges will definitely improve our mood. Giving energy to all the good that is happening in the present seems quite impractical and tough. Nevertheless, it has been proved to be useful in many cases as it elevates the soul and works on the person internally.

The incident of 'wrong job' that I have discussed in length at the beginning of this chapter had a deep and significant impact on me as it was my first job. It sowed within me the sensations of deep regret and resentment. I had doubts about my decision-making ability and feared to make one lest the same pattern repeats. At first, the very thought of this incident had such a negative impact on my mind that my temper levels would shoot up, and I was termed 'very difficult'. The anger for failing myself burst forth as being curt and overbearing. This phase continued for many years until I realized its effect on all my relationships, and I wanted to change myself.

One principle that I have inculcated from my mom right from childhood is that no matter how intense the situation is, change is always possible and inevitable. Verily, this principle holds a deep, spiritual inner meaning which I have been able to infer to a great extent. However, the younger me took this principle on face value and made it the truth of my life. I always believe that we can change at any moment provided we are ready to pay the price for it.

The idea of *change* begins in the mind, and it is all a mind's play. Once I decided to make changes, the first thing I did was to accept that I am a human being who makes mistakes. I stopped being overly critical of myself instead, I chose to use the time wisely to pay close attention to my career interests. I started working on enhancing myself to suit my pursuits and also made sure to revive my relationships with my loved ones. The ' wrong job' was a one of a kind incident that taught me a lot. Undoing the damage was an uphill task but I believe that I succeeded to a great extent in setting things right in all aspects.

"The self-work that you do in silence will echo throughout every part of your life." - Michell Clark

I know that it is easier said than done, but the point is, do we have a choice??? Being accountable for our deeds is so much better than lamenting and crying over what is lost. I agree that a lot of dedication and steady effort needs to be put in the initial stages. We may be under the impression that we are fooling ourselves by indulging in all these mindless practices and these techniques will not work for us. We think that out there in the world there are a *specia*l few who are blessed and given extraordinary powers. But friends, this is surely not the case. If I can do it, so can everyone.

By embracing these changes with a broad mind, we can expect to receive the hidden blessings that are waiting right at our doorstep to present themselves into our physical environment. We not just grow by years but evolve into wiser and prudent individuals. Our outlook towards people and the community as a whole begins to gradually alter. We set about pursuing and seeking occasions to celebrate and rejoice. At this moment, this may seem as being way far from the truth. Barring a few gut-wrenching incidents, all others may be given a pass and damage control is certainly possible in those cases. Assiduously working towards a positive mindset is the first step in our advancement.

I would like to summarize that it is easier to make amends in our present and obtain the results as we had envisaged. Speculating about the time to come, which is far and uncertain, leaves us asking for more. A lot of continued practice and diligence goes into nurturing constructive thoughts despite our present hardships. It is no mean feat to adapt and navigate through the hardships with our heads held high as we march towards our intended goal. By merrily experiencing every second thoroughly, we are well-equipped for a deserving and bright future that is awaiting us with open hands.

CHAPTER TEN

THE BALANCING ACT

Every phase that a person is in comes with its own responsibilities and challenges. Obviously as we grow older, it is expected from every one of us to don more hats and take accountability for our actions. All of us know that from the moment we wake up in the morning until going to bed we are confronted with a number of trials in every sphere that shape us as a person. It is of utmost importance to maintain a fine balance while fulfilling all our roles as tripping in one direction may have a major impact in the other arenas as well.

I am very well aware that the mere thought of managing and delivering results is in itself quite overwhelming. We all know that the term **'work-life balance'** is extensively used in recent times. There is a very delicate line that keeps our personal and professional lives apart. It is this *line* that makes all the difference. There are many times when I get bogged down by all the works that I am expected to complete. I don't know which ones to prioritize, and which to postpone for a later date. I suppose that everyone would affirm that a slight slack or faux pas from our end could aggravate our situation further.

" Balance is not something you find; it is something you create."

At this point, I would like to discuss one such episode that put me in a tight spot and thereby taught me a lot. There was a presentation at office that was very crucial for me as my performance in the presentation would decide the future course of my career. I knew how important *that day* was going to be for me and so I put in a lot of effort after the office hours. I used to work late in the night after finishing all the household work and after putting my daughter to sleep. Though I was drained out completely, I continued working on my project and somehow managing my other responsibilities as well.

During the course of my preparation, I found it very difficult to cater time to my daughter that I normally used to do. Seeing me always being preoccupied and on the run made her adamant. She was too young to figure out the reason for my behavior and the only way she could gain my attention was by being stubborn. Though I knew in the depths of my heart the real cause for her misbehavior, I refused to let it go. The stress I was in further compounded the already tense scene spoiling the atmosphere at home. Though I calmed down and later pacified my daughter, my intuition indicated in clear terms that it was time I put things in order, else everyone may have to bear the brunt for it.

The date for my presentation was fast approaching and I was focusing more on that, shooing off the warning signal that I had received. I thought to myself that once all the works at office get successfully completed, I would shift my focus entirely to the activities at home. Unfortunately, that never happened, and everything went for a toss. I believe that the underlying tension with regards to my work clearly reflected in my actions messing up the ambience at home. I failed to draw clear boundaries and had to pay a heavy price for it. Unfortunately, the presentation didn't go as expected and that made me feel even more pathetic.

This incident occurred a long time ago when I was not aware about the concept of freewill. Ever since I have learnt about freewill, I make sure to use it wisely whenever I am at a crossroad in my journey. Another mistake that added to my woes was that I neglected and overlooked my gut feeling due to the pressure I was in. I didn't take the required action at the right time despite the repeated alerts worsening the scenario. I understand that it is not always possible to define and set demarcations with respect to our responsibilities. We do end up losing focus and screwing up everything around us. But giving up is never an option to set matters straight and get things back on track. On the other hand, effectively using our freewill and acting based on our intuition can help us to reroute the direction of our trail towards abundance.

Just because we slip and fail to fulfill our duties doesn't mean that we are not good enough. As mentioned in Chapter 4 – Acceptance of Oneself, every problem can be fixed the moment we accept ourselves with all our drawbacks. Doing so immediately diverts our attention from the problem to finding ways to solve the issue at hand. I wish to point out that blaming ourselves for our incompetence in handling the situations with finesse will only amplify our tensions. Instead at this stage, we need to open our hearts to self-love and be gentle with ourselves. When we view troubles as obstacles that help us grow as individuals, then success is no longer a distant dream.

CHAPTER ELEVEN

PARENTING

The idea around parenting has progressed over the years and there is a lot of difference in the way it is perceived in recent times. Parenting can be viewed as an act where a subtle balance needs to be maintained for the process to fructify. There are multiple facets to the central concept of parenting, that invariably renders the people involved asking for more. I believe that the upbringing strategies used by the previous generations are more or less irrelevant in today's world. The main reason that the earlier parenting methods seem outdated in recent times is because there has been a major shift in the mindsets of modern-day parents.

Parenting is an everyday task that requires continuous fine-tuning depending on the need of the hour. This implies that it is not a one-time activity and only adhering to a particular set of principles may not work at all times. We all know that walking on the edge of a cliff needs focused and renewed attention just in case we lose our balance. Coincidentally, the same holds good for parenting to be effective and give us a favorable outcome. We all have heard our elders teaching us that there is no shortcut to success. As a parent, I presume that this premise of triumph fits correctly to the basic idea of parenting.

The actual process of parenting is akin to how we plant the seeds in soil and water them intermittently with lots of care. We nourish them with fertilizers and maintain the optimum temperature so as to enhance their growth. The fertilizers that we choose and the temperature to be maintained depend on what seeds we have sown. Some seeds may require *that* extra attention and focus in comparison to others. In much the same way, a lot of nurturing and care is mandatory for parenting to be successful in **its right sense**.

I would like to emphasize the phrase 'in its right sense' and elaborate on it a little. The aim of doing this is because victory is relative and cannot be judged from a single person's viewpoint. For each individual, the success rate with respect to the ideology of parenting is varied and I deem it is absolutely valid. When we are not hard upon ourselves for our faults and instead look for ways to get out of the issues bothering us, we are for sure making a headway. When we begin to seek alternative solutions our feat as parents is unquestionable and undeniable. As we open our hearts to better prospects, new paths and ideas start to show up.

"There is no such thing as being the perfect parent."

Parenting is not a *'one-size-fits-all'* means as was followed in the past. Back then, the psychology of the child was most often ignored, and all the children of the house were bucketed into the same group. As a matter of fact, while growing up my parents treated my sisters and me in the same way, even though we were so different as individuals. Parents in those times did not essentially recognize that there is a possibility of every child in the household being different. Once we get hold of this pivotal clue, the path traversed from there on gets both interesting as well as fruitful. I would like to make it clear at this point that I do not wish to show any disrespect to parents of the previous generations and personally do not intend to hurt anyone's sentiments.

Every person in this world is unique with different skill sets and talents. The same holds good for a childas well but most often than not, we as parents tend to overlook this finer aspect. The reason for this is that we think that we know our child very well and are only working towards their best interest. There is no doubt in our intentions as it known that we try every possible means to keep our children happy. We all know that in some cases, parents stretch themselves both financially as well as psychologically. This is a very familiar scene in many families, and I am sure that everyone reading this will agree with my views.

Every child is special and unique by birth. This makes it all the more important to nurture them based on their distinct nature. Some may need that additional support while others may not need it *at that point of time*. I would like to focus on the phrase '*at that point of time*' that is specified in the previous sentence and discuss its significance. When I say, 'at that point of time' it implies that for that instance or phase of time the child is in a position to manage things by himself/herself. I am of the perception that children need to be closely observed for changes in their behaviors. Once we witness any inappropriate or unusual conduct , we may have to enter the scene and take charge of the situation.

As a mom to my nine-year daughter, I am no exception to this. My daughter always keeps me on my toes with her choices and ideas. I find her unpredictable and whimsical. It is very normal for any kid to have varied interests – all at the same time when they are in the age group between 3 years to 10 years. The prime cause behind this can be attributed to the fact that it is during this time that the child explores the world - in their own way and at their own pace. Though I am cognizant of this and acknowledge it , at times my eclipsed reasoning nudges me to push my daughter to focus on one activity so that she can pursue it further. Despite reminding myself often that she needs to be given her space so that she can blossom effortlessly, I stumble off the track.

Most of the time, I am left fuming and scratching my head in disbelief as her trail of thoughts are in complete contrast to my ideas *for her*. She incessantly surprises and astonishes me by her reasoning capabilities. There are many times when my daughter and I have conflicts because of our contrasting thought processes. As a protective parent, I tend to think that she is too young to make correct decisions but that is not always the case.

"The uncertainty of parenting can bring up feelings in us that range from frustration to terror."

I am aware that the way I have been brought up will not work for my daughter. I am certain that there is every chance that she will not be able to resonate with it and find them old-fashioned. I regularly have face-offs with reality that shake me up completely and put me into the thinking mode again. I begin to analyze how effective I am as a parent and self-evaluate my concept of upbringing. We may claim several times that we are open to change and willing to incorporate new ideas. But the question that every parent should ask themselves is - Are we *really* open to trying new ways of parenting that suit our case and be reasonable in the process or not?

All of us have a template on parenting readily available with us that has been handed over to us by our loving parents and grandparents. However, putting it into use as it is without evaluating it adequately will not bring in the expected rewards. It may not help the situation as expected and there is every possibility of it further weakening our existing relationships. In most cases, a slight change here and there is just enough, whereas in other *special* cases we may have to create an entirely new template from scratch. When we conceive this new template (most often we do it mentally), we need to bear in mind that it is a customized one specifically for our child.

When we look at parenting from a responsibility standpoint, then for sure it becomes a boring drill. I have learnt in my journey as a mother that being a parent doesn't always have to be a tough and rigorous task. It can be turned into a fun-loving activity at times. However, I do understand that it is not always possible but surely, we can give it a try. I would like to credit my husband for helping me through this and making me realize that parenting doesn't need to be strenuous. We engage my daughter in fun games while sitting in the car waiting for the traffic to clear (Chapter 3 - Concept of Freewill) and sometimes also ask her for suggestions with regards to an outing that is in the works. She promptly starts planning our trip and gets totally involved in it. By doing this, we ensure that she gains confidence to execute a task and doesn't shy away from putting her thoughts into action.

These are some of the many activities we keep her busy with. These not just keep her cheerful and in high spirits but also alleviates our tensions owing to the daily errands. It distracts us and awakens the inner child within us. There are innumerable such occasions where we have got solutions to our lingering problems when we were having a joyous time as a family. As we begin to enjoy the time spent with our kids, it becomes instinctive without our knowledge. In the interim, we form a beautiful and intricate bond with our children that cannot be articulated. Though all these ideas give the impression of being preachy, I think that it is best if every parent gives it a try at least once. I am confident of the results as I have personally got success by modifying my style of parenting depending on the circumstances.

There have been many such instances where I did not ascertain the situations in the right manner and my predictions went haywire. All of us want to safeguard our child's future and tirelessly work for it. This truth cannot be disputed at any cost. By doing this we get so involved in it that we unknowingly end up wanting to *gain absolute control* of our child's life. Most of the time, we are unaware of this and not careful about our actions as parents. We often neglect and fail to pay heed to our behavior with regards to our children. When we keep the traits of our child in mind and prioritize their needs as well as opinions, it is highly unlikely that we overpower their lives.

What I mean to say by the phrase – 'gain absolute control' is that we disregard the suggestions put forth by our kids citing being young as a reason and miss out on a number of important aspects pertaining to our children. In many situations, we shoo away the children and shut them off claiming that we are doing everything for their own benefit. We begin to start deciding every single thing for our children under the pretext of being protective. However, unfortunately we pass over our doings as the responsibilities of parents and take every possible opportunity to prove ourselves right. We start to live our child's life and impose our interests on them.

At this point in our book, I request everyone to take a pause to evaluate and assess our actions as parents. By introspecting the bond that we share with our kids once in a while, we learn where we stand in our role as parents. This self-analysis done at regular intervals of time is very essential and productive as it facilitates us to fix issues that crop up in the initial stages itself. Whenever we notice that my daughter's behavior is changing or we sense discomfort in her body language, we know for certain that it is time to get back to the drawing board for further introspection and analysis. A parent-child relationship is a very pure bond that is centered on the ideas of trust and confidentiality. Just like all the other relations in the world, even this interconnection is a two-way association where the responsibility as a parent is huge.

Understanding a child and knowing a child are two entirely different theories. But sadly, we mix them up and take offense when as parents we are called out for our decisions. Understanding a child means that we put ourselves in their shoes and perceive things from their stand. We try to examine the situations from their point of view and work as a team with them for plausible solutions. Doing this has a twofold advantage – the first benefit is that it opens the lines of communication between the parents and the children, and secondly our outlook is broadened.

Transparency and a non-judgmental attitude are the secret ingredients to any healthy relationship. When we take the time to calmly understand the child's prerogative, we begin to observe that the child is no longer holding back his/her views. By letting the child speak out, we try to drive into the child's mind that his/her views are being heard and valued. This action on our part may seem as minute but it is not so. This small yet significant act from our end infixes into their innocent minds loads of self-confidence and self-worth. Only when we trust our kids with their decisions, can we expect them to confide in us and ask for our opinions.

"Behind every young child who believes in himself is a parent who believed first."

Teaming up with our kids and spending quality time with them relieves us from our everyday load. It lightens our soul and opens our mind's eye to the limitless happiness that can especially be seen *only* from a child's angle. Parenting done in the correct way, with the right intentions, hardly faces obstacles. It not just ensures that a thriving kinship between the parents and children exists but also fosters a healthy rapport between them. Additionally, we discover the innumerable manners in which a scheme can be worked out provided we are open to learning and receiving knowledge from our kids.

So far, we have addressed extensively how understanding a child rightly is advantageous to both the parties concerned. There is a subtle yet striking difference when parents say that they know their child very well. This reminds me of a very funny incident that left me embarrassed but schooled me to keep my mind open. I noticed that my daughter was spending a lot of time in crafts and coloring. Whenever she had leisure time, she kept herself busy with oil pastels and color pencils. This caused me to conclude that she loved hues and shades. I thought that if I get her enrolled in a painting class, it will help her hone her craft and thereby improve her skills. Thinking in this way, in a state of excitement without discussing with any one I got her all the materials that she would require for her class. However, when I showed her everything, she showed least interest in any of them. When I questioned her about it, she revealed that she was into the coloring activity as she had nothing else to do. It was out of boredom that she was doing it.

I felt abashed and thanked the stars for not getting her enrolled in the class without comprehending the situation correctly. I was not just saved from the monetary loss but also from the displeasure that would have spoilt the ambience at home, had I gone ahead with my half-cooked plan. Thrusting our expectations on the kids without taking the effort to understand them in the true sense is in vain. It only strains our bonding with the children to an extent where getting things onto track may be quite harrowing and onerous. Letting our children down by not respecting their choices is a sure shot recipe for disaster.

I fully agree that no relationship is devoid of imperfections and issues. Nonetheless, it is upon us to not let the dissatisfactions outweigh our relationships. Just as there is a gestation period for the seeds implanted in the soil to germinate, in a similar manner the parent-child bonding unfolds slowly and steadily over a period of time. Do we dig up the soil again and again to see if the seed is growing or not? Surely, not. On the contrary, we take adequate care to speed up the growth of the plants by watering and nourishing the seeds properly. In exactly the same way, we need to re-evaluate and re-calibrate our style of parenting from time to time to align it with the needs of our child.

Having open discussions with children about their career or personal choices enhances the good vibe and creates a cheerful, vibrant atmosphere at home. Healthy conversations in the confines of a home among family members have proved to be of great help to everyone concerned. It opens up a bunch of new opportunities which were till then unexplored. Whenever we have conversations with our loved ones with the thought process to identify solutions, newer horizons open up. We are astounded at the various perspectives that exist which we never even knew. However, that is only possible if we are open to alter our stance on subjects galore.

Healthy and constructive conversations between parents and children raise the level of intimacy even further. Every child secretly wishes that their parents stand up for them and support them unconditionally. As a child and even during my growing years, I have always wanted my parents to have confidence in me and trust my decisions. It was my belief that if my parents approved of my choices then it meant that I was on the right path and my success was assured. I didn't understand the depth of this feeling then, but now when I try to analyze the hidden emotions within me it gives me goosebumps.

I think that it is perfectly normal for a child to have such strong, deep-rooted feelings. The main reason for this is the unique nature of the parent-child connection where the child looks up to their parents for everything. This is the way a child's mind works and as parents, it is our responsibility to be aware of this vital point. *Just by being there for them* whenever they need us, we uplift their morale. All of us are bound to make mistakes in different stages of our life and there is nothing wrong in it. Bearing the genuineness of this statement in mind, even children should be given a benefit of doubt and a chance to express their points.

However, it would be a blunder if we don't rectify them at the correct time. As parents, we should be big-hearted enough to accept our children despite their shortcomings and flaws. Drawing comparisons can prove to be quite detrimental and barely motivates the child. On the other hand, there is every possibility that the child would get into a shell and gradually lose confidence. Instead of calling out the children for their lapses, working along with them in the direction of their goals is obviously more valuable and profitable. Despite the fact that I have put forth these views about parenting, I do take impulsive decisions and end up jumbling things. However, I strongly opine that quickly making the necessary changes by admitting the mistakes made, lessens the stress and is probably the easiest way of damage-control.

CHAPTER TWELVE

Conclusions

In all the chapters that have been depicted so far, we have spoken about the different angles of our life that we run into daily. This chapter rightly titled **'Conclusions'** servesas a befitting conclusion to all our learnings in a nutshell. The biggest takeaway from this chapter is that it will help us connect the dots we have seen so far. Every chapter given in this book has deeply buried lessons that are waiting to show up in our physical world. Once we identify the missing elements and place them in appropriate locations, we get the complete picture of our dreams that is tailored *especially* to suit our needs. We all are aware that every one of us is distinct and so are the experiences we face.

If we take the initiative to transform ourselves depending on our situations, I can ascertain one and all that it is just a matter of time before avalanches of abundance will flood our homes. There are multiple interpretations to the word 'Life' . This means that there are a number of standpoints from which its basic definition can be decoded. From the moment where we are able to perceive things, most of us (if not all) always strive to achieve a grandiose lifestyle. There is no denying the fact that a majority among us are in awe of such abundance and magnificence. When we measure our results in terms of luxury, it means that we have succeeded in fulfilling *only* our materialistic needs.

Another interesting dimension that is clearly mentioned in the book in Chapter 2 - Life and Spirituality is the premise of spirituality. I am reiterating the fact that all of us are spiritual beings who have taken physical birth on planet Earth so as to enjoy our sojourn here. This state of tranquility is revealed to us when we are at peace with ourselves. When we have the right school of thought and an inquisitive frame of mind to grasp ideas that may seem illogical initially, knowledgeable ideas work out by themselves. As we joyfully take pleasure in our ride and immerse ourselves in deciphering our quest, every desire that we had secretly wished for, begins to unfold so beautifully. Words fail to describe the love with which we are caressed and taken care of during our tough times by a power that is invisible but very well existent. How soon we accept this self-evident truth and benefit from this, is entirely at our disposal .

"The only impossible journey is the one you never begin." - Tony Robbins

When our Life spirals downward and everything around us seems to be disintegrating, that is *indeed* the perfect time when we need to cling on to the hope that the storm will pass off sooner than expected. During those tiring moments, we are preoccupied and in mental anguish due to our conditions that we start to feel powerless and hopeless. The sad news is that when trouble conceals us from all sides, we often waste our energy on such low-vibe thoughts that pull us down even more without realizing how harmful they are. It is in rough weather that the actual personality of an individual shows up. The one who stays unruffled in the middle of the tornado is compensated heavily as opposed to those who are ready to give up at the drop of a hat.

I wish to remind all the readers of the amazing power of freewill that can help us get out of troubled waters successfully. In Chapter 3 - Concept of Freewill, we have extensively reviewed how efficacious freewill is. On a higher level, it is just a vague idea. But when we take it upon ourselves to dive in all the more to gather more information, we are left wondering at its power. Freewill is but an intangible concept that needs to be cultivated and worked upon. It is a skill that requires constant refining and tuning in order to stay relevant. We are tested as it were, but if we can reignite and regain our internal strength in taxing situations, good times cannot elude us for long. Time is all-changing, and happiness when it comes in, is sure to sweep us off our feet.

Spirituality and Personality Development go hand-in-hand. Showing enormous mental strength in exacting times is a sign of a strong personality. I was always of the opinion that a spiritual being is one who seeks solace in the mountains and engages in endless prayers. However, I have learnt that it is a myth and every one of us is a spiritual being - the difference only lies in the level of consciousness and self-control among the people living in this world. People who break down easily may require a lot of inner work to be done but it is not something that is impossible. I hope to end the book on a high note with a strong belief that every one of us can surely fix the pieces of our life into their right positions provided we have the right attitude .

It has been stated by Napoleon Hill that we realize that our Life is a Do-It-Yourself Project only after more than half our duration is completed. When I stumbled upon this quote, it not just made so much sense to me but also made me feel so safe and secure. I convinced and reassured myself that I am not the only lone wolf in this scary jungle. There are many of us who are rambling aimlessly and need a guide who can safely take us to our destination. I have put forward my ideas on paper with the single intent of helping everyone through some of the learnings that I have carefully picked along my rocky adventure. I desire that the methods and techniques given in the book serve as a beacon in dark times. By firmly clasping on to them we can get on with our travel having the least fear in our minds.

"It doesn't matter where you are coming from. All that matters is where you are going." - Brian Tracy

Sometimes it is our own expectations that hamper our growth as we are forever criticizing ourselves for the mistakes we make. We are not ready to admit that failures play a major role in enhancing us as an individual. Success and failures are two sides of a coin and the sooner we understand it, the better for us. The more we resist this idea, the more forcefully it bounces back on us leaving us in shattered pieces. Failure is a reality that needs to be accepted and by welcoming this idea with an open heart we change the basic foundation on which our life stands. Just as a building built on a solid foundation stays firm and grounded in all weather conditions, in a similar fashion it is the correct mental outlook that makes all the difference.

When we begin to view failures as a medium of scrutiny that have been intently sent to uplift us, we can be rest assured that we are treading towards an enchanting future. This is a huge thought process change that is strikingly contrary to our normal reactions when we are wrapped up in anguish and commotion. Failures are not obstacles that have been placed on our path purposely to block us. Instead, they have come to teach us to ignite the fire within ourselves and continue on our path of growth. When we accept disappointments as a must-have, key ingredient in developing our identity as a whole, it means that we have understood the true meaning of being here. Our approach automatically changes, and we begin working our way towards a flourishing, positive outlook.

"Good things come to those who wait."

Most of the time, we are in the pursuit of learning new concepts to improve ourselves with no in-depth understanding of how to implement them in the right way. I am restating the same lines over and over again - Life is not a competition that needs to be won, but a tour that should be experienced. We need to bear in mind that none of the concepts discussed in this book to better our lives are *quick-fix solutions.* I presume and lay stress on the pivotal point hinted subtly in the book. All the tools enlisted in the preceding chapters have a significant influence on us as a person if put into proper practice. They reinforce the power of self-worth in us, and consequently we gain a better insight into our well-being.

Frankly speaking, a certain measure of dedicated and consistent effort is definitely needed on our part to start noticing visible improvements. The time span for any process to fructify varies from person to person. Our labor should be directed and focused in a set route rather than being scattered. Focus is the primary component that summons favorable outcomes. When we set an intention and work relentlessly in that direction, success is assured. Triumph and victory become our constant companions. Regardless of the occurrences in our environment, our aim should be to put our best foot forward. This may, at a glance, startle us given the fact that we are all human beings with emotions. When we make it our second nature to not react absurdly in a state of torment, calming down will automatically follow in line and become our subsequent step.

"Good things take time."

Research studies divulge that a timespan of a minimum of 21 days (some say 30 days) is required to rewire our thoughts and beliefs with respect to any particular ideology. I assume that the above explanation provides relief as well as answers to many of our readers who are constantly bugged by a nagging question – why is there no change in ***my*** life? Only when we stick to *one* particular approach for at least 21 days and take maximum efforts in that direction, can we be sure of observing positive changes in our wellness. As we stretch ourselves to the maximum limit with the altruistic purpose of spreading happiness our life prospers manifold.

On the other hand, when we try our hand at all the *new* concepts that are highly spoken in the market we end up in a soup. Our scattered and messy attention draws mixed results that are in no way close to our expectations. The actual problem in this case is that in an attempt to get faster rewards, we do not even bother to take the effort to digest the ideas properly, let alone master them. When we keep swinging between different ideologies, we confuse our minds to a large extent with all the knowledge available on the internet. We literally dump every possible piece of matter into our minds in a frantic and desperate move to achieve quicker results.

By forcefully trying to put everything into use, we overwhelm ourselves needlessly. We fear that our time is running out and we may miss our train. Comparing our lives with others worsens our condition even more and affects our mental health too. Though we have lots of information available with us, we lack the clarity to put it into effective use. Everything is only perceived in the form of bits and pieces by our brain due to ambiguity. The prime reason for this pitiful condition is that there is nothing concrete and worthwhile. We can do nothing but regret for putting ourselves in a fix.

All of us know that half-knowledge is dangerous and by trying every possible technique available inconsistently, we land ourselves in a half-baked situation. Our half-cooked knowledge is not just useless, but also gives us the impression of being pulled in all directions and invariably we feel lost despite being surrounded by our loved ones. Instead of identifying the cause of our pathetic state, we boldly claim that all these self-development methods are futile and worthless. To top it, we conclude that everything is a gimmick, and none of this ever works!!!! If we had bothered to persist a little longer with our drill, we would have profited in more ways than one.

I suggest that instead of baffling ourselves with techniques and procedures, our options should be based on our requirements. We should make choices that best fit our situation. It is not wrong to try out the techniques to test their efficiency. Nevertheless, every solution that has been proposed in the book takes a minimum of 21 days to even start showing minor results. I do not by any means claim that we can achieve overnight success by adopting these changes into our daily routines. I also request the readers not take on the mass psychology in this aspect as it may end up as a failure and prove fatal. When we go to and forth between multiple alternatives just because others are doing it without realizing our true necessities, we may not get the expected profits.

It is always encouraged to take on life as it comes - one moment at a time as constant comparisons and self-expectation only serve as hindrances in our treasure hunt. It increases our anxiety levels and brings on uninitiated ego clashes. All of this may seem far from reality and misleading. Nonetheless, as we ponder on the learnings that I have portrayed in this book without being judgmental, I am confident of the inexplicable internal bliss all of us would experience.

When we quiet the wheels of our mind by keeping ourselves away from all the chatter of the world, we are rightly guided by our internal guidance system (Chapter 4 - Acceptance of Oneself). The instant we become conscious of the fact that life is not just about winning or losing , our entire focus shifts onto our journey instead of on the intended goal. Our priorities change and we begin to walk on the track before us with aplomb. As long as we keep the candle of hope alive within ourselves, there is light at the end of the tunnel.

Towards the end of the book, I urge everyone to always be on the lookout for improvement. Let there be no complaints about God being unfair *only to us* because that is never true. Once we take its reins into our hands there is no looking back. Our aim should be *only* to seek happiness at all costs and always be high-spirited despite the outer circumstances. Being pinched off when confronted by unexpected provocations will only aggravate the situation and once again everything goes downhill.

Life is like a book where every chapter is bound to be different. As we intently study every page of our book and assimilate its spirit, we become ready to face the next chapter. It is just a matter of time before we find ourselves drenched in our aspirations that is **now** a reality. The premise of life is moving forward and none of us is an exception to this. If we are able to perceive this statement in the right sense, then no one can stop us from achieving our dreams and goals. As we start treasuring our adventurous ride, Magic starts to unfold effortlessly and its charm echoes everywhere.

Resources

1. Ask and It Is Given : Learning to Manifest Your Desires –

   by Esther and Jerry Hicks (The Teachings of Abraham)

1. The Secret – by Rhonda Byrne

3. Think And Grow Rich – by Napoleon Hill

4. 40 to 40 million – by Dr. Anjanaa Reetoria

5. https://www.youtube.com/watch?v=qGW1XOehMmU&list=PLwaL5mlt8L2yKAggKnHP-oh2sU1rPpl6w

6. https://www.youtube.com/watch?v=lZq6J_k2BIg&list=PLwaL5mlt8L2yKAggKnHP-oh2sU1rPpl6w&index=5

7. https://www.youtube.com/watch?v=GK3JVkw-tgw&list=PLwaL5mlt8L2yKAggKnHP-oh2sU1rPpl6w&index=27

8. https://www.youtube.com/watch?v=KXj7tk9Peq8&list=PLwaL5mlt8L2yKAggKnHP-oh2sU1rPpl6w&index=41

9. https://www.youtube.com/watch?v=ukpEtWxOki0

10. https://www.youtube.com/watch?v=sGtz66bhYzk&list=PL-JMyu1gMqtdW4NaVpsXAXaGlVI1__fQw&index=22

www.ingramcontent.com/pod-product-compliance
Lightning Source LLC
LaVergne TN
LVHW021200160826
845679LV00024B/2187